Life-Giving
LEADERSHIP

"*Life-Giving Leadership* is a tool every woman in leadership should have in her tool belt. Reading it will encourage you to seek healing from hurt and disappointment and step into your full potential as a life-giving leader. The wisdom Julia shares has the power to transform the lives of women and the church as a whole."

—**Stephanie Blanton,** LifeGroups coordinator and volunteer coordinator, Freedom House Church

"This information on life-giving leadership has transformed my thinking and revolutionized the way I look at leadership. Leadership is not a set of rules to follow, but a freeing, encouraging, and supporting of the people in our spheres of influence. Julia has encouraged me greatly in my walk with Christ and in my leadership role."

—**Cheryl Moore,** women's ministry leader, Bayside Community Church

"Julia's writing compels and motivates me to become a more life-giving leader. I am confident her book will be an excellent resource for women seeking to lead with the life-changing nature of Christ."

—**Mary Reed,** women's ministry leader, counselor, and life coach, Chapel Presbyterian Church

"You can always count on Julia to listen more than she speaks, but when she speaks the words are always full of discernment, wisdom, and truth coupled with real-life encouragement that leaves you feeling a tangible inspiration of how to move forward."

—**Jacqueline Zdrojowy,** Awaken Church

"Julia's book displays deep wisdom and a tender heart to see women come into their own and land where God has already designed a place for them."

—**Kamla Long,** Director of Discovery Seminars

"Julia's writing is a unique blend of inspiration and practical application. As I read *Life-Giving Leadership*, it challenged me to examine how I can be more intentional and life-giving!"

—**Kristin Bonham,** women's ministry Director, Grace Family Church

Praise for

Life-Giving Leadership

"I'm thrilled that Julia Mateer, who has already impacted so many women with her refreshing counsel and leadership, has now given us her written tool so that many more can be inspired."

—**Christa Hardin,** Owner and Director of Reflections Counseling Center

"*Life-Giving Leadership* comes from a place of experience and authenticity. As books for Christian women seeking to lead begin to increase in number, this one will be a book that you will keep on your shelf and return to again and again."

—**Karen Zeigler,** author, speaker, and Founder of National Association of Christian Women Leaders

"What a great book full of insight and inspiring stories on how to become a life-giving leader. Julia will fuel a passionate desire in your heart to become the leader God has called you to be."

—**Kim Anderson,** Director of Women's Encounters

"As a licensed mental health therapist and pastor, Julia very aptly demonstrates how life events can hinder us from reaching our full potential as leaders. She will keep you engaged from beginning to end as she guides you through overcoming hindrances in order to develop a life-giving character that will minister to others."

—**Marsha Champion,** Missions Coordinator, Bayside Community Church

"From the authentic stories to the questions to dig deeper, this book reels you in and takes you on a personal journey. Free people free people, and I believe this book is going to lead to a ripple effect of women getting free and reaching into the fire to free others!"

—**Erin Blair,** co-pastor of Limitless Church

"Julia Mateer gently yet dutifully guides you in the evaluation of your emotional and spiritual health. With the voice and wisdom of a mentor, she will nurture and equip you to become the life-giving leader God has designed you to be."

—**Jenni Catron,** author of *The 4 Dimensions of Extraordinary Leadership*

Life-Giving LEADERSHIP

A WOMAN'S TOOLBOX FOR LEADING

JULIA MATEER

LEAFWOOD
PUBLISHERS
an imprint of Abilene Christian University Press

LIFE-GIVING LEADERSHIP
A Woman's Toolbox for Leading

LEAFWOOD
P U B L I S H E R S
an imprint of Abilene Christian University Press

Copyright © 2016 by Julia Mateer

ISBN 978-0-89112-341-5

Printed in the United States of America

Published in association with The Blythe Daniel Agency, Inc., PO Box 64197, Colorado Springs, CO 80962.

Many of the scenarios in this book are compilations of various stories gleaned over years of ministry. Unless indicated, names and identifying details have been changed to protect the privacy of individuals.

Cover design by ThinkPen Design, LLC
Interior text design by Sandy Armstrong, Strong Design

Leafwood Publishers is an imprint of Abilene Christian University Press
ACU Box 29138, Abilene, Texas 79699

1-877-816-4455 | www.leafwoodpublishers.com

16 17 18 19 20 21 / 7 6 5 4 3 2 1

This book is dedicated to my treasure,
Caroline Hope. You are my dream come true.
May you always live and lead out of the tree of life!
Listen to the One that has called you and
passionately live out his adventure.
It's a great gig!

Acknowledgments

I first want to thank the ultimate Helper, the Holy Spirit. Without his love and faithfulness to me, this book would not exist.

To Mark, there are no words to describe the depths of my love for you. Thanks for all the encouragement, laughter, and prayer support. I am your number one fan as you are mine. What did I do to get such a good man? Only by his grace, that's for sure.

Joseph and Shawna, Phillip, and Caroline, you are my treasures. I hope this book makes you proud.

To all my cherished friends who have encouraged and supported me through the writing and publishing process, you are the best!

To my Bayside Community Church family . . . wow . . . doing life with you makes life so sweet. It's what dreams are made of . . . so grateful for my church.

Finally, to Blythe Daniel, the best literary agent on the planet, who kept pressing on with this book until it found a home at Leafwood Publishers; my heartfelt thanks to Blythe at Blythe Daniel Agency and Mary Hardegree and team at Leafwood Publishers. What a joy it's been!

Contents

Foreword

I first met Julia at a roundtable for women in ministry leadership. It was clear from the first time she spoke that we both shared a passion for seeing women become rooted, grounded, and free in Christ, and go on to fulfill their potential in him. I listened to her talk about this desire throughout the few days we spent together at the event, and I was so impressed by the wisdom she possessed— wisdom she delivered in practical terms in a spirit of grace without compromising truth.

A year later, when I was getting ready to publish my own book, Julia was one of the people I asked to read my manuscript and give feedback on my treatment of the complex subject of the human soul. I had not known Julia long, but I immediately realized that she was someone whom I could trust, and who could also provide guidance as I wrestled with some of my own ideas. Julia came through. Her insight was just what I needed to finish strong and stay on the right path to complete the rest of my book.

Imagine, then, how delighted I was when Julia asked me to write the foreword to her book. Even more than that, I was delighted to find that she had taken all that wonderful passion, wisdom, and practical advice and channeled it into a book. As I read the manuscript, I could sense the same heart attitude of grace and truth that I felt when I first met her.

In *Life-Giving Leadership,* Julia draws upon her own story as well as her many years of practice as a mental health therapist and experience as the small groups pastor in her church. Her journey has endowed her with a treasure trove of knowledge, understanding, solid insight, and practical application. But most importantly, perhaps, these experiences have gifted her with an undeniable empathy and compassion for those who labor under the weight of hurt and confusion. This pain is magnified when people come to church to find hope, but find judgment and rejection instead.

It is a tragedy that such an experience has come to characterize the stereotypical portrayal of the church. Unfortunately, such a caricature continues to be perpetuated because all too often the church is unequipped to handle the timid overtures of those who tiptoe through her doors looking for refuge. That is why *Life-Giving Leadership* is a necessary book.

As leaders in the church, we are aware that we are commissioned to go into all the world and make disciples. But what happens when those "future disciples" walk through our church doors? In our zeal to honor the Word of God and protect the purity of the church, we can sometimes fall into the trap of equating rejection of sinners to faithfulness to God. And yet, Jesus Christ, the perfect example for faithfulness, welcomed sinners into his company for the very purpose of extending grace to them. How can we, sinners redeemed, do anything less radical? And yet, we do.

In *Life-Giving Leadership*, Julia gets right to the heart of the matter, which is, actually, the heart of the leader. It is possible, she says, to be spiritually saved, but emotionally stunted. To be passionate about correct behavior and doctrine, but apathetic or downright hostile to the people our example and doctrine are meant to impact. The solution, as Julia explains, is to move from an outside approach to one that works from the inside through the transforming work of the Holy Spirit. Walking alongside you as only someone with her experience can, Julia will take you though the steps of healing needed to bring wholeness and life on the inside so that they overflow into your relationships, your ministry, and your world.

So many people want to be leaders—they sense the call to something that will allow them to have an impact on the lives of others. That is a noble desire and a good thing! But the weight of leadership will crush the divided soul. A divided soul riddled with unforgiveness, insecurity, or past wounds, will collapse under the strain of pulling others up. To lead for the long haul, we must first lead ourselves to wholeness and strength. In this wonderful book, Julia gives you the tools to become whole and strong and to stay that way.

I believe that *Life-Giving Leadership* will not only bless you, but will also be a valuable resource to those who serve under your leadership. I know that once you begin this journey to life, you will never be the same!

For His Cause,
Kerri Weems

1
. . . .

The Life-Giving Difference

"Neither do I condemn you." —Jesus

Catching my eye, a woman sporting a bouffant hairdo and wearing a polyester-pleated skirt walked toward me. Placing her body close to mine, she bent down and whispered, "Don't you know you are doing a striptease with that dress?" "Excuse me?" I said, not believing what I had just heard. She repeated her observation. I mustered a weak "thank you."

Staring straight ahead, I questioned myself. *What was wrong with this dress? What was wrong with me?* Pulling my dress down to cover as much of my legs as possible, I desperately yearned to go back to campus and never set foot in a church again.

Why are some Christians life-giving, while others suck the life right out of a room? I believe the answer lies in knowing and understanding grace. Life-giving people are God lovers, and because of this great love, they are people lovers, too. A Christian who focuses on right behavior and right doctrine strangles the breath out of relationships. A life-giving person focuses on the love and grace of the Lord Jesus Christ, and understands that people are more important than right behavior and right beliefs. Relationship trumps rules and law.

In 1980, Ronald Reagan was president. *God and Country* appeared on billboards and bumper stickers nationwide. "Who shot J. R.?" was the question on everyone's mind. I was an eighteen-year-old college student hungry for an authentic relationship with God.

Organized religion had failed to ignite an encounter with the Creator; in fact, it had almost snuffed out the flame, but a spark deep within me still smoldered. On a quest for God, I wasn't sure what to do or where to go. I felt a visit to a local church was a logical starting point; however, my experience in church as a little girl tempered my expectations.

Around the age of nine, I received the *Living Word*, an easy-to-read Bible. I would lie on my bed and read the Gospels. I read the encounters of Jesus healing the sick, feeding the hungry, and casting out demons. I knew the Bible said in John 14:12, "I tell you the truth, anyone who believes in me will do the same works I have done, and even greater works, because I am going to be with the Father."

Because I took the Bible literally, I went to one of the pastors at the church I attended. I asked her why I didn't see at church what I had read in the Bible: healings, feeding the hungry, and casting out demons. I don't remember the pastor's answer. I just remember it wasn't adequate for my curious mind and childlike faith. Even at a young age, I was searching for something real and authentic and, instinctively, I knew I hadn't found it at church. From then until the time I was nineteen, I didn't step into a church again.

Because of my experience as a child, I knew religious protocol dictated that a dress was the appropriate attire for Sunday church. Wanting to fit in, and not wanting to embarrass myself, I bought a muted purple, cotton dress with small slits on each side so I could sit properly.

For weeks, I had observed a set of twins on campus who dutifully went to church wearing skirts and carrying their Bibles in quilted covers. These girls appeared to have a connection to God—perhaps they could plug me in. They didn't even have to proselytize me. I was willing and wanting to attend church with them. So I asked if I could ride with them to church. They were surprised but eagerly agreed to my request. On Sunday morning, I put on my new dress and went to church with the twins. I hadn't slept the night before due to a growing anticipation of the spiritual experience I was hoping I would have.

Approaching the main entrance, my eyes wandered back and forth, trying to lock onto something familiar or at least a friendly face. The pews were hard, the service was solemn, the people looked miserable. Internally, I was uncomfortable but trying to keep an open mind. Eventually, we stood up to sing the fourth stanza of the last hymn of the service.

Finally, the pastor directed the crowd to a large room called the fellowship hall. Crossing my legs, I sat at a table with the twins. I noticed a group of women leaning against a wall, glaring at me. Even though it was the '80s and big hair was in, these women took big hair to the next level, with bouffant hairdos and polyester-pleated, below-the-knee skirts. They each wore white blouses with cardigan sweaters. I diverted my eyes so they wouldn't notice I was staring. And then it happened, the encounter with the bouffant-polyester woman.

Feeling judged, embarrassed, rejected, and angry, my quest for God went on hiatus that day. I was on the precipice of making a commitment to Christ, but I was turned off and shut out by the self-righteousness and pride of the women at the church.

Now let's compare my experience with that of a woman named Tina.

Feeling the shift of the weight in their bed, Tina knew her husband had left her side. At midnight he climbed out of their bed, quietly shut the bedroom door, and went into their office. Keeping the lights off, he logged onto his computer and began his nightly routine of conversing with a woman he had met online. He had been "chatting" with her for the past five months and was contemplating meeting her face-to-face.

Knowing something was going on, Tina quietly followed him into the office and came face-to-face with his secret. He jerked around, realizing he had been caught, his eyes locked on hers. Tina screamed, "What are you doing? Is it what I think? Tell me the truth."

After hours of arguing and crying, her husband took a deep breath and let it slide out. "You don't get me. She does." The sad reality was that her husband was done. As the night turned to morning, the shouting became whispers, the interruptions became long, painful pauses that seemed to last forever. His last words were, "I'm sorry." Determined to end his marriage, he packed a bag and left the home they had shared for nine years.

Sitting on the side of her bed, Tina covered her face with a cool cloth as waves of emotional pain swept over her stomach, causing nausea and vomiting. She didn't know what to do. With racing thoughts, she wondered if she should call her mom and tell her what had happened or if she should run after him. Tina was smart enough to know that if she didn't reach out for help now, she would be swallowed up in self-pity for days.

She remembered a card she'd received the previous day that was in a stack of mail on her dresser. The card advertised a new church in the area that offered hope and an opportunity to connect with God and people. Picking up the card, she flicked it back and forth between her fingers, wondering what to do. Church had never been a part of her world, but her world had just crumbled, and she was willing to take a risk, hoping the card would deliver on its promises.

She went to her closet and picked out the nicest dress she owned—a "club" dress that she wore when she went out with her girlfriends. She didn't know and didn't care if the dress was appropriate. She just wanted help. And now, with sweaty hands and a pounding heart, she turned the car into the parking lot. Having never stepped inside a church, she was not sure what kind of people she would find. Would they judge and criticize her, or would she find the help that the card advertised?

Turning the engine off, she took a deep breath and slowly walked up to the front doors. She was greeted by several people who seemed genuinely happy to see her. She was then escorted to the main auditorium where she chose to sit in a row close to the back doors in case she wanted to make a fast getaway.

The stage lights came up and the crowd stood to their feet. Tina followed suit. Music filled every inch of the room, and it was not churchy music, either. It sounded just like the music she heard on the radio, but the words spoke of God's love and grace. She began to relax and give herself to the experience, and soon she found herself weeping. The message spoke to her thirsty, broken heart.

Sitting next to Tina was a woman named Lilly. Lilly had experienced an unwanted divorce, causing her intense pain and heartache. Lilly was wise because she took her pain to God and allowed him to work his healing in her heart. Her experience with divorce made her sensitive to women in emotional pain. She noticed the tears in Tina's eyes, and she asked if there was something she could do for her. Tina was surprised and touched by the woman's kindness, making her cry even more. Tenderly, Lilly escorted Tina to the lobby where she listened as Tina poured out her story. Lilly prayed for Tina and committed to call her the next day.

Walking out the same doors she had come through earlier, Tina felt encouraged and comforted. Gone were the sweaty palms and anxious heart. Tina couldn't really explain what had happened internally to her, but she knew she felt differently. Somehow, some way, she felt hopeful and accepted. In the back of her mind, she thought how glad she was that she came to church today.

As she drove away, she remembered a phrase she heard in the message: "No matter how deep your pain, God is a God who heals." She couldn't wait to speak with Lilly about this God. Receiving a glimpse of God's love and grace through Lilly, Tina left feeling hopeful and accepted, not condemned or rejected.

Lilly is a wonderful example of a life-giving woman. Having experienced the love and grace of the Lord Jesus Christ, she extends grace, mercy, and love to those around her. Her focus is on an intimate relationship with the Lord Jesus rather than on the law or rules. Lilly was a woman filled with purpose and intentionally went to church looking for the Tinas of the world. Some services they came and some services there was no one. But Lilly always made herself available to hurting women. Lilly knew that on this particular day, Tina was not there by accident, but God had intervened in Tina's life and had propelled her into a new direction.

The love and grace Lilly extended to her produced hope in Tina's heart. The bouffant-polyester woman focused on the rule of appropriate dress, which produced shame and condemnation. Lilly focused on connecting with Tina rather than on what she was wearing. Lilly understood the important truth that no one will listen to you unless they feel that you like them. If someone perceives that you don't like or approve of them, then what you believe, think, or say will have no impact or influence in their life.

Now imagine for one moment what the scenario could have looked like if the bouffant-polyester woman had been life-giving in her interaction with me. What if she had noticed me sitting at the table waiting for lunch and had approached to introduce herself, asking about my life instead of judging my appearance? If that woman had extended love and grace instead of judgment and criticism, my experience in church would have been vastly different. Instead, she missed an opportunity to impact a young woman's life for Jesus.

Life-Giving Encounters between Jesus and Women

Tina resembles another woman who was desperately seeking help. You find her story in the Gospels (Mark 5:21–43; Matt. 9:18–26; Luke 8:40–56). Tired and weak, this woman had endured bleeding for twelve years. She had spent all of her money seeking help from physicians and still was unable to find a cure. Hearing that a man named Jesus could heal the sick, she desperately wanted to find him. After searching for him, she found Jesus in the midst of a crowd. Pushing her way toward him, she extended her hand and touched his hem. At that very moment, she began to tremble and knew that she was healed. Instinctively, she fell at his feet and told him her story. Jesus said to her, "Daughter, your faith has made you well; go in peace and be healed of your affliction" (Mark 5:34 NASB). Like Tina, she experienced hope, grace, and love.

Another woman, desperately in need of help, was pulled out of a room and into the street as the men looked forward to her stoning. She was caught with a man who was not her husband. Taken to Jesus, she was sure her life was over, but instead she found life and not death, grace instead of judgment, love instead of shame. Jesus's final words to a broken and promiscuous woman were, "Go and do not sin again." There was no judgment in his words. Her sexual activity was not a secret to Jesus. They both knew what she had been doing. Yet the words "neither do I condemn you" took the condemnation away, filling her with hope. If there was judgment to be found, it was in the hearts of the self-righteous men who brought her to Jesus hoping to stone her to death. Rather, they came up against love personified and scattered away.

The woman experienced healing because of this life-giving encounter with Jesus.

And finally, we find Jesus speaking to a Samaritan woman about issues of the heart. Sexual customs and prejudices were eradicated by Jesus when he spoke with her. The Bible says that Jews had no dealings with Samaritans, let alone a Samaritan woman. He revealed that he knew of her five marriages as well as her current relationship. Astonished by his revelations of her life, she became a Christ follower and influenced many in Samaria to become followers as well. John 4:39 says, "From that city many of the Samaritans believed in Him because of the word of the woman who testified, 'He told me all the things that I have done'" (NASB). Because Jesus was *the* ultimate advocate for women, each life-giving interaction between Jesus and these women ended in something positive: freedom, healing, and conversions.

His genealogy is dotted with women who lived outside of societal norms for their time and culture. Women such as Tamar, Rahab, Ruth, and Bathsheba brought such things to his history as incest, prostitution, adultery, and interethnic marriage, which was forbidden in that culture. Author and psychologist Dr. Diane Langberg writes,

> Jesus arrived as the seeming illegitimate son of a virgin in a culture that should have stoned her because she was very much outside the parameters. She did not maintain her role or place in that society. . . . He went from there to swim

upstream by saying things like, looking on a female as a sex object is the equivalent of adultery (worthy of stoning in that culture). He began His ministry by blessing an unnamed bride in Cana. Women publicly traveled with Him, a stunning and offensive situation in that culture. He treated one woman as a male disciple when He affirmed her presence at His feet and treated another as an apostle when He paused in His work of saving the world to raise a girl-child from the dead, returned a son to a widow and brother to two grieving women. He accorded women dignity, honor, safety, education and privilege.[1]

We see example after example of Jesus encountering women, but the reality for us in the twenty-first century is that he isn't physically walking on the earth today. He is seated at the right hand of the Father. "When the Lord Jesus had finished talking with them, he was taken up into heaven and sat down in the place of honor at God's right hand" (Mark 16:19). However, you and I and the Lillys of the world are here. Tina experienced the love of Jesus Christ that day because Lilly was willing to be his hands and feet. Just like Jesus was willing to encounter the woman at the well, Lilly was willing to hear Tina's pain.

Just like Jesus, we, too, can be effective advocates for women by providing life-giving leadership to the women we lead. Being a life-giving leader begins with being a life-giving person, and to become life-giving, you must first be born again (John 3:3). Once you have a relationship with the Lord Jesus, you have the choice to live out of the tree of life and the finished work of the cross, or the tree of knowledge of good and evil and the law where there is condemnation and a sense of failure in God's presence.

What is the tree of life? It is first mentioned in Genesis when God had to remove Adam and Eve from the Garden of Eden because they ate from the tree of knowledge of good and evil. Once they ate from that tree, sin entered mankind. There was also the tree of life in the Garden of Eden. If Adam and Eve had eaten from the tree of life with their sin nature, they would have lived forever. For this reason, they had to leave the garden, and God placed cherubim and a flaming sword to guard the tree of life.

Genesis 3:22–24 says, "Then the LORD God said, 'Behold, the man has become like one of us in knowing good and evil. Now, lest he reach out his hand and take also of the tree of life and eat, and live forever—' therefore the LORD God sent him out from the garden of Eden to work the ground from which he was taken. He drove out the man, and at the east of the garden of Eden he placed the cherubim and a flaming sword that turned every way to guard the way to the tree of life" (ESV).

All of Scripture can be summed up in the basic principle of love. God is love, and you were created to experience intimacy with your heavenly Father and with people in the context of community. There is nothing more normal than to deeply love God and others. Our goal as life-giving leaders is to extend grace and mercy to the people we lead, to encourage them to have an intimate love with the Heavenly Father.

One cannot be spiritually mature and life-giving without being emotionally healthy, and emotional health is rooted in a healthy self-esteem. Having an accurate, honest, and appreciative perception of oneself is the basis of healthy self-esteem. Glenn Schiraldi writes in *The Self-Esteem Workbook*,

> If you want to have self-esteem, it helps to choose your parents well. Children with self-esteem tend to have parents who model self-esteem. These parents consistently are loving toward their children, expressing interest in their child's life and friends, and giving time and encouragement. I am reminded of the man who said to his neighbor, "Why did you spend all day with your son fixing that bike, when the bike shop could have fixed it in an hour?" The neighbor replied, "Because I am building a son, not fixing a bike."[2]

Parents of children with healthy self-worth have high standards, show clear and reasonable expectations, and give support and encouragement. The child feels loved, respected, and valued because his or her opinions, gifts, and talents are valued and considered; however, parents make final decisions of importance by sending a message of security to the child. Building healthy, secure attachments is imperative in developing emotionally healthy children.

How do we help people have an intimate love with the Father when we struggle to know and understand love ourselves, since many of us have been wounded from unhealthy family relationships? The secret to life-giving leadership is emotional health. Emotional health or the lack of it manifests in interpersonal relationships. Those who are emotionally healthy are friendlier, more expressive, confident, self-trusting, trusting of others, and less troubled by mental health issues and criticism. When someone is emotionally unhealthy, he or she becomes self-focused and selfish, rather than other-focused.

There are countless numbers of people who are emotionally healthy but are not Christ followers. However, they are incapable of being spiritually mature because they don't have a personal relationship with Jesus enabling them to experience the transformative power of the Holy Spirit. However, there are many Christians who are emotionally unhealthy, which inhibits their spiritual maturity and inhibits their ability to have life-giving, functional relationships.

I believe that people can be emotionally mature but not spiritually mature unless they know the Lord Jesus; however, many believers are stunted in their spiritual growth because they aren't emotionally healthy. One cannot be spiritually mature without being emotionally mature, and emotional maturity lies in the heart of a life-giving believer.

For example, the bouffant-polyester woman's emotional immaturity inhibited her from accepting me, a young girl visiting her church, seeking an encounter with the living God. Criticalness and judgment oozed out of her. There are several reasons for stunted emotional growth and emotional immaturity. Here are a few:

- Poor parenting or the absence of a parent, resulting in abandonment issues.
- Insecurities resulting from a weak sense of self-identity or self-worth.
- Sexual, physical, or emotional abuse.
- A catastrophic event in a young child's life, such as a death of a loved one or divorce.

So what are we to do if our backgrounds include one or several of the incidences mentioned above? People who are life-giving, emotionally mature, and able to love others freely have experienced the love of God. They understand that the love of God is a safe place for their hearts. Experiencing the love of God empowers you to forgive yourself and others. Forgiving others empowers you to love others unconditionally.

Life-giving leadership is embedded in love and begins within and is manifested in our relationships with those we lead. To unlock the mystery of love, just look at the healthy relational principles listed in 1 Corinthians 13:4–6: "Love is patient and kind. Love is not jealous or boastful or proud or rude. It does not demand its own way. It is not irritable, and it keeps no record of being wronged." Applying these principles to our leadership creates healthy, life-giving relationships, which in turn create healthy, life-giving churches that attract the unsaved, the uncommitted, and the unchurched.

Emotional health begins with understanding love. To authentically love people, you must first understand that your experience of love colors how you love others and God. Our life stories determine our ability not only to give love but also to receive love. Our "love receptors" can be healthy or unhealthy. So, following are some valuable questions to ask and explore with a trusted mentor or counselor.

- What is my story of love?
- How did I learn to give and receive love?
- What occurred in my childhood to inhibit my ability to receive and give love?
- How does this affect my current relationships?
- How does this affect my ability to experience God's love?
- What lies do I believe about love? For example, say your father walked out on your family. You may equate love with abandonment. Who wouldn't? That would be a reasonable conclusion for a child to draw because our parents are our first teachers about love. These lies become embedded in our souls and soul-wounds occur and our love-receptors become skewed. We will discuss how

to heal from the collateral damage of these lies later in this chapter.

Like many women, I suffered from low self-worth because of childhood experiences. My journey toward self-love and emotional maturity began with an understanding of God's love for me—that I could bring all of my junk to him and lay it at the cross and find grace in my time of need. I had a significant breakthrough in my internal atmosphere when I understood the truth that *Julia is the righteousness of God in Christ Jesus* (see 2 Cor. 5:21). I began to practice his presence, basking in his love, by meditating on Scriptures about his love for me.

> And I am convinced that nothing can ever separate us from God's love. Neither death nor life, neither angels nor demons, neither our fears for today nor our worries about tomorrow—not even the powers of hell can separate us from God's love. No power in the sky above or in the earth below—indeed, nothing in all creation will ever be able to separate us from the love of God that is revealed in Christ Jesus our Lord. (Rom. 8:38–39)

> For God so loved the world, that he gave his only Son, that whoever believes in him should not perish but have eternal life. (John 3:16 ESV)

> Give thanks to the LORD, for he is good! His faithful love endures forever. (Ps. 136:1)

Jesus replied, "The most important commandment is this: 'Hear, O Israel! The Lord our God is the one and only LORD. And you must love the LORD your God with all your heart, all your soul, all your mind, and all your strength.' The second is equally important: 'Love your neighbor as yourself.' No other commandment is greater than these." (Mark 12:29–31)

Imitate God, therefore, in everything you do, because you are his dear children. Live a life filled with love, following the example of Christ. He loved us and offered himself as a sacrifice for us, a pleasing aroma to God. (Eph. 5:1–2)

Not only did I meditate on the truth of his love for me, but I also sought out Christian counseling. It is amazing the healing that occurred in my life when I was willing to unclothe my pain, dig beneath the surface, and allow a real transformation to occur within my mind, will, and emotions. Having a Christian counselor work through this process with me was invaluable. If your heart resonates with my story, I would strongly encourage you to connect with a Christian counselor and let the healing begin. Your path to becoming an emotionally healthy, life-giving leader like Lilly is right around the corner. So, are you a bouffant-polyester woman or a life-giving Lilly? Let's do a self-assessment. Using a scale from 0 to 10, "0" being the least and "10" being the most, put a number between 0 and 10 beside each characteristic.

Bouffant-Polyester Woman	Life-Giving Lilly
____ judgmental, critical, focuses on right behavior	____ focuses on grace and love
____ focuses on the law and rules	____ believes relationships trump rules
____ sees God as an angry task-master	____ sees God as a loving Father
____ repels people	____ attracts people

Don't worry if your scores were lower than you'd like. The goal of this book is to help you become a life-giving follower of Christ so you can influence the women you lead to fall deeply in love with Jesus Christ. In the next chapter, we'll begin by looking at the characteristics of a life-giving leader.

Small Group Discussion Questions

The Life-Giving Difference

1. Discuss your first experience in church.

2. Have you ever felt judged in a church setting?

3. Who would a newcomer walking through the doors of your church encounter? Would she encounter life-giving Lillys or bouffant-polyester women?

4. Discuss your reaction to Jesus's interactions with women in the Bible.

5. What do you think of Julia's assertion that Jesus was *the* advocate for women?

6. What are your thoughts on Jesus's genealogy, including several "trashed" women—Tamar, Rahab, Ruth, and Bathsheba? What message does this list send to the broken women you encounter in your ministry?

7. Brainstorm strategies to create life-giving environments in your local church for women.

8. What does it mean to be life-giving?

9. Discuss the difference between the tree of life and the tree of the knowledge of good and evil.

10. Which tree do you lead from?

11. Discuss how you can be more life-giving in your interactions with other women.

12. Can you relate to Lilly or the bouffant-polyester woman?

Notes

[1] Diane Langberg, "Where to Now? Women as a Mission Field," *Christian Counseling Today* 13 (2005): 50.

[2] Glenn R. Schiraldi, *The Self-Esteem Workbook* (Oakland: New Harbinger Publishing, 2001), 19.

2

Characteristics of Life-Giving Leaders

You may be asking yourself, "What does it mean to be life-giving?" A life-giving person is someone who lives her life by focusing on the love and grace of the Lord Jesus Christ versus living her life by the law. A woman who seeks to be a life-giving Christ follower is attractional and moves people toward a relationship with Christ, but when a Christ follower focuses on right behavior, on how someone should act or be, she drives people away from Christ.

The purpose of this chapter is to help us understand what it looks like and feels like and how it plays out in our daily lives to lead out of the life-giving nature of Christ. To help us better understand this paradigm-shifting concept, this chapter will focus on the characteristics of life-giving leadership.

A Life-Giving Leader Knows God Determines the Atmosphere of Her Soul

Have you ever been around a woman going through great personal trials, and yet she gives herself fully to the people around her, never showing an inkling of distress or pain? She has found the secret to sustainable joy: a life-giving leader knows that Jesus, not the circumstances of life, is the One who determines the atmosphere of her soul. I know of two such women. Both of these women, greatly respected by their peers, have known extreme physical pain and lost dreams. Their lives have been fraught with difficulty and yet their souls are at rest, enabling them to pour out grace and mercy to others. Here are their stories.

Rebecca

Twenty years ago, Rebecca and her husband, Paul, moved to a multilevel home in Genval, a beautiful part of Belgium, to continue their lives' call of gathering people around Jesus through church plants and house churches. Their influence and relationships spanned continents including North America, Africa, and Europe, filling their days with counseling, listening, speaking, and leading.

On this particular morning, she was leading a small group of parliamentarians' wives, which she loved to do. She understood that making guests feel welcomed was a way to honor God and positioned the atmosphere for her guests to be able to hear from him. Rebecca was a woman who loved to serve God by serving others. Much like Lilly in our first story, Rebecca's desire was to minister to others. She understood that the heart of life and its joy is in relationship with God and with others. Her daily prayer was, "Father, how do you want to use me?" This day was no different.

As the small group was coming to a close, Rebecca gathered the empty teacups and plates. Placing them on a tray, she descended the stairs to the kitchen with the dishes, and for unexplainable reasons, Rebecca blacked out and fell, making no attempt to catch herself. Upon hearing a loud crashing noise, Paul, who was working in his office, and the women from the small group in the upstairs sitting room ran to find Rebecca at the bottom of the stairs with her head badly bent back. She wasn't breathing and had no pulse.

At that moment, the cleaning woman who was studying nursing instructed Paul to do mouth-to-mouth resuscitation while she did CPR. The ambulance arrived and rushed Rebecca to the hospital. The diagnosis was a break in her neck at the second vertebra, rendering her a quadriplegic. Unable to move or breathe without a respirator, Rebecca was at her darkest hour.

After five and a half months in ICU, several surgeries, and another fourteen months in a hospital rehabilitation facility, she was finally released to go home. Rebecca's life became drastically different with undesired and painful challenges. Her prison was a wheelchair and her particular paralysis required round-the-clock care. Rebecca's life was now one of dependence on others for her basic needs.

At their darkest moment, Rebecca and Paul chose to embrace the love, grace, and mercy of Jesus that they had known and preached throughout America, Africa, and Europe. Rebecca knew that God, not her circumstances, determined the atmosphere of her soul. Until the end of her life in January of 2014, Rebecca encouraged believers to find joy and contentment in the middle of terrible loss and pain, living the truth that Jesus empowers us to endure the unendurable.

You may be wondering: How does someone who has endured so much pain and loss find peace in her soul? I believe there are steps that we can take to help us press on and come to a place where, like Rebecca, God determines the atmosphere of our souls.

Allow yourself to go through the processes of loss. Rebecca didn't come to a place of peace overnight. Once she processed through the anger, pain, and loss of her situation, then she could begin the next steps.

Give thanks with a grateful heart in every circumstance. First Thessalonians 5:18 says, "Be thankful in all circumstances, for this is God's will for you who belong to Christ Jesus." It is important to note that thankfulness is *not* the same as resignation. Giving thanks brings God into the situation. Thankfulness puts our hearts on him and not ourselves.

Use your pain to bless others. Letting go of our dreams—whatever they are—frees us to live in his daily presence, being about his will for us and not our own agendas. It frees us from discontentment and allows us to pick up his plans, purposes, and ministry for our lives. Lilly did not choose for her marriage to end in divorce any more than Rebecca chose to be a quadriplegic, but they both purposed to use their pain to bless others.

Mary

Having led many retreats, the platform was a comfortable place for Mary as she found herself once again sharing about God's truths to a room full of women eager to learn more about Jesus and his Word. She was smiling and ever encouraging, and the women in the room would never know that Mary suffers daily with debilitating migraines exacerbated by fibromyalgia.

Mary, a small, petite woman, began having migraines at a young age. For most of her adulthood, she has sought treatment for her headaches without much success. Many of her days are spent managing pain, and often her nights are spent sleepless. She has tried different diets, acupuncture, traditional and nontraditional medications, and Botox. Nothing has brought relief.

Like the woman who bled for twelve years who could find no earthly cure, Mary has not been able to find any treatment, diet, or medication to stop the migraines. Her healing has been a continual focus of prayer for those of us who know and love Mary. Mary had a choice. She could have allowed her circumstances to determine her purpose and call, or she could press into Jesus, receive his grace, and pursue his plan for her. She chose to allow

God, not her circumstances, to determine the atmosphere of her soul.

Just like Rebecca, Mary is often called upon to listen, pray, counsel, speak, and lead. But so many days it is hard to get out of bed. The searing pain in her head makes it difficult just to get in the car. It would be much easier to shut down, to lie on the couch, and to sleep the day away. What if Jesus had decided to pass up the cross because it was too painful, too hard, and too difficult? What if he had decided to pass up the cross and go fishing?

Here is what we need to understand: turning your pain into ministry enables you to move forward in life so that you are not defined by adversity. Allowing God to use you to minister to others becomes a beacon of hope and encouragement to those in pain. Thinking that our problems disqualify us from being used by God keeps us trapped in a cage of isolation, rendering us useless in reaching out to bless others. The extent to which you allow God to heal you is the extent to which you will be able to help others.

Women like Rebecca and Mary are my heroes. Most of us don't deal with half the pain they struggle with. Most of us were up late last night watching a movie and now we're too tired to attend church or small group. Whenever I am tempted to whine or complain, I remember their stories and say to myself, "Julia, put your big-girl panties on, and get your butt in gear!" Then I get about my Father's business, remembering that it's not about me.

Life-Giving Leaders Are Led by the Spirit

A life-giving leader understands the difference between being led by the Spirit of God and being driven out of an unmet need. A ministry or church that is personality-driven is usually led by a person who has a deep need for approval stemming from a fear of failure and rejection. A prevailing sense of worthlessness is often manifested in ministry by a need to achieve, perform for God, and win the approval of Christians, generating a "rock star" complex. The apostle Paul warns us in Philippians 2:3–5, "Do nothing from selfishness or empty conceit, but with humility of mind regard one another as more important than yourselves; do not merely look out for your own personal interests, but also for the interests of others. Have this attitude in yourselves which was also in Christ Jesus" (NASB).

There are inherent dangers in a personality-led ministry. People can become focused on the person rather than on Jesus. A person's gifting, though God-given, can be distorted by arrogance and pride rather than through yielding at the cross.

The measure of a life-giving leader is not in the quality of teaching she shares or the prophetic word that she gives or even the number of hours she prays. It is found in the fruit that is manifested in her life when she is behind closed doors. James 3:17 says, "But the wisdom from above is first pure, then peaceable, gentle, reasonable, full of mercy and good fruits, unwavering, without hypocrisy" (NASB).

God created each of us with intimacy needs. According to Dr. David Ferguson and Dr. Don McMinn, we each have ten intimacy needs.[1] Here is a list of the top ten intimacy needs from their book, *Top 10 Intimacy Needs*:

1. **Acceptance**—deliberate and ready reception with a favorable response (Rom. 15:7).
2. **Affection**—to communicate care and closeness through physical touch (Rom. 16:16).
3. **Appreciation**—to communicate with words and feelings a personal gratefulness for another (1 Cor. 11:2).
4. **Approval**—expressed commendation; to think and speak well of (Rom. 14:18).
5. **Attention**—to take thought of another and convey appropriate interest and support; to enter into another's world (1 Cor. 12:25).
6. **Comfort** (empathy)—to come alongside with word, feeling, and touch; to give consolation with tenderness (Rom. 12:15).
7. **Encouragement**—to urge forward and positively persuade toward a goal (1 Thess. 5:11; Heb. 10:24).
8. **Respect**—to value and regard highly; to convey great worth (Rom. 12:10).
9. **Security**—confidence of harmony in relationships; free from harm (Rom. 12:16a).
10. **Support**—come alongside and gently help carry a load (Gal. 6:2).

When these needs are not met, soul-wounds can occur and a prevailing sense of worthlessness may develop. When affirmation is missing and intimacy needs are not met, performance becomes the basis of self-worth. Believing the lie—that love is about what she does, rather than who she is—a leader may crave love and acceptance from God and other Christians. Driven to lead, she seeks approval through spiritual achievement and ministry success. Meeting a need for affirmation and approval, women's ministries can be used by leaders as a source of identity. Jane is a perfect example of a woman who developed a soul-wound that negatively impacted her leadership.

Jane

Jane grew up in an alcoholic family where emotional and verbal abuses were an everyday occurrence. None of the ten emotional needs were met by her parents. Her father was rarely home, and when he was, he barely spoke to her. Overwhelmed by his responsibilities and his wife's drinking binges, he isolated himself from the family.

Jane's mom was drunk most of the time, so Jane was left to care for herself with no one to love and encourage her. Often she would come home and find her mom in bed. With no one to greet her, ask her about her day, care about what she thought or felt, or hear about her dreams and plans for the future, her childhood was lonely.

Since her intimacy needs were not met at home, Jane found a way to get her needs met through unhealthy relationships with boys. Eventually she married twice, with both marriages ending in divorce. She simply wasn't equipped for relationships that required healthy emotional attachments. She sought approval through her job performance, which drove her to work fifty or more hours a week. Her emotional insecurities caused an anxiety disorder which led to binge eating, causing her weight to drastically fluctuate.

One of Jane's co-workers invited her to church, and it was at this service that Jane experienced the love of Jesus and became a Christ follower. Ecstatic at the love she felt from her new relationship with Christ, she threw herself into the activities of her local church. The pastor was eager to give some of his responsibilities away, especially when it came to women's issues. So Jane became the women's ministry leader. Her need to perform drove her to devote countless hours of ministry with little to no personal boundaries.

After working tirelessly to develop a conference, her unmet needs for affection and acceptance surfaced when some members of her leadership team challenged a few of her ideas at a pre-conference meeting. Jane blew up at the women, accusing them of sabotaging the conference and ruining all of her hard work. The women left deflated, unheard, and angry. Eventually, they stopped volunteering with the women's ministry, finding other areas in the church to serve. In reality, these women had legitimate concerns and were trying to have an honest and open conversation with Jane. But because of her soul-wounds,

Jane perceived their concerns as criticism, triggering her unmet intimacy needs, and she responded out of insecurity and fear.

Suppose Jane had worked through her unmet intimacy issues in counseling or with pastoral oversight. The meeting may have looked like this: the women present their concerns about some of Jane's ideas for the conference. Jane, desiring to provide life-giving leadership to her team, listens intently to their concerns, validates the team by thanking them for their hard work, and acknowledges how hard it can be to bring concerns to a leader. The group has an open and honest dialogue about the conference, and everyone leaves feeling heard and appreciated. Each woman stays a part of the team and continues volunteering within the women's ministry.

If you recognize yourself in this scenario, and you have realized that a soul-wound is driving your need to lead and minister, then ask yourself this question: "Am I leading because I am being led by the Spirit, or am I leading because it fills a need to be loved and gain approval?" If your answer is yes to the latter, please understand it's easy to read this in a book, but it's hard to recognize in the moment. Soul-wounds can be healed, but it takes being honest with yourself, humility, and the willingness to change. The following are steps you can take to heal your soul-wounds.

Share with a mentor. Talk openly about your issues with your spiritual authority such as your pastor, an elder, or a spiritual mentor. James 5:16 says, "Confess your sins to each other . . . so that you may be healed. The earnest prayer of a righteous person has great power and produces wonderful results."

Seek counseling. When you receive counseling from a trained professional, you don't have to worry about that person sharing your issues. HIPPA laws protect your confidentiality. Make sure that the professional counselor approaches therapy from a Christian perspective.

Have an accountability partner. An accountability partner is someone you can trust. She isn't afraid to call you on the carpet, hold your feet to the fire, and encourage you to move forward. Hebrews 10:24 says, "Let us think of ways to motivate one another to acts of love and good works."

Seek prayer support. There is a plethora of Scriptures encouraging us to pray for one another. Second Thessalonians 1:11 says, "So we keep on praying for you, asking our God to enable you to live a life worthy of his call. May he give you the power to accomplish all the good things your faith prompts you to do."

Step away from leadership. This step takes great self-awareness, humbleness, and maturity. If necessary, for your sake and for the sake of the women you lead, step away from leadership and give yourself the gift of time to let the healing begin. This doesn't mean that you will never lead or minister again; however, it does mean that you will be able to minister to others from a healthy emotional and spiritual place. So, what would stepping away look like? Many leaders who have needed to step away take an agreed-upon sabbatical, perhaps six months or a year. During this year, it is recommended that you receive therapy to work through the emotional challenges that hinder your ability to have healthy relationships, as well as rest. Resting, both physically and emotionally, is restorative to both your body and soul. Also, finding hobbies that bring you joy brings balance to your life.

A Life-Giving Leader Knows That Pain Is Part of the Gig

Sitting in the cold bleachers, the adrenaline flowed as the gates opened and the horses flew out of their stalls. Eyes were plastered on the chestnut thoroughbred with the jockey in red as they plunged to first place at least seven lengths ahead of the pack. Just like the horse out in front, a position of leadership puts you out front for all to see, watch, and judge—bringing pain and heartbreak. That is why so many pastors' children choose *never* to go into full-time ministry, because they have witnessed firsthand what the dark side of leadership can bring to marriages and families: scrutiny, criticism, gossip, and rejection.

Pain is part of leadership. A great example of this is found in the story of Joseph in Genesis 37–48. Driven by jealousy, his brothers threw Joseph into a cistern and then sold him into slavery. From this point on, Joseph endured great suffering, persecution, loneliness, imprisonment, shame, and grief. Eventually, God rescued him and placed him in a positon of leadership, influence, and authority as the ruler of Egypt, second only to Pharaoh.

An integral part of Joseph's story is the choice he made to forgive his brothers and provide food for them during a great famine. We find a glimpse of his pain in Genesis 42:23–24: "Of course, they didn't know that Joseph understood them, for he had been speaking to them through an interpreter. *Now he turned away from them and began to weep.* When he regained his composure, he spoke to them again. Then he chose Simeon from among them and had him tied up right before their eyes" (emphasis mine). The Bible doesn't talk about it, but I can imagine that Joseph had to guard his heart.

Understanding that pain is part of leadership, a life-giving woman understands the necessity of guarding her heart. Here is Ella's story.

Ella

It had been three months since Ella, director of life groups at her church, heard crying coming from beside her bed. She woke to find her teenage daughter lying beside her. Ella remembered how her heart pounded and a panicked feeling came over her; something was terribly wrong. Her daughter lifted her head and looked into Ella's eyes. "I'm pregnant, mom. I'm so sorry." Sitting straight up in her bed, Ella knew the way she handled this moment would determine her relationship with her daughter for the rest of their lives. Ella remembered putting her hand on her daughter's back, lying back down beside her, and crying. No words, just love. There would be time to talk in the morning, plus Ella had known she needed time to process the news and pray.

For Ella, that moment seemed like a lifetime ago. After learning about her daughter's pregnancy, Ella and her husband told their pastor, who was also Ella's supervisor. He responded exactly as she knew he would—with grace and mercy. But not everyone at the church was as understanding. Walking down a corridor of the church, Ella overheard two youth group volunteers disparaging her daughter's character and Ella's parenting skills. Their words insinuated that Ella's daughter should have known better, especially because Ella was on staff. This was one of several painful encounters Ella endured over the next several months. Ella was keenly aware of the truth of Proverbs 4:23: "Guard your heart above all else, for it determines the course of your life." She knew she needed to guard her heart, or she would fall straight into a pit of bitterness. Perhaps Ella found herself in the same place that Joseph found himself when he was sold into slavery by his brothers.

A life-giving leader knows that she does not have the luxury of closing up shop and going home just because she gets "kicked in the rear," her feelings get hurt, or she gets criticized. The challenge is to resist hardening your heart and quitting the race. The tendency is to give up and stop engaging in life—to put our jammies on, curl up in a blanket, and eat chocolate when we are struggling and feeling defeated—but a life-giving leader presses into love, takes another risk, and embraces another relationship. First Corinthians 10:13 states, "The temptations in your life are no different from what others experience. And God is faithful. He will not allow the temptation to be more than you can stand. When you are tempted, he will show you a way out so that you can endure."

This is exactly what Ella did. She went to her pastor and processed through the pain she was feeling and was able to forgive those who had hurt her and her daughter. Ella refused to take herself out of the race. She continued to love others and engage in people's lives. She pressed into love and continued her race. Ella stood on his promise found in 1 Peter 5:10: "In his kindness God called you to share in his eternal glory by means of Christ Jesus. So after you have suffered a little while, he will restore, support, and strengthen you, and he will place you on a firm foundation."

The greatest tactic of the enemy is to get you to stop loving and ministering to others and to retreat to where it is safe . . . out of commission and out of life. Is the answer to resist forming attachments to people? Do we cease trusting, loving, or committing because someone might hurt us? Do we run and hide from love because our hearts may get broken? Do we give up on our passions, dreams, and goals because our hope wanes?

I wonder what would have happened if Joseph had become bitter. Would his family have perished from starvation? Life-giving leaders know that disappointment, conflict, and pain is part of life, and to close our hearts because of the possibility of pain is to close our hearts to life.

Like Ella, we must maintain a forgiving heart toward others to keep our heart life-giving and soft. Jesus said in Mark 11:24–25, "I tell you, you can pray for anything, and if you believe that you've received it, it will be yours. But when you are praying, first forgive anyone you hold a grudge against, so that your Father in heaven will forgive your sins, too." The writer of Hebrews warns us in verse 12:15, "See to it that no one comes short of the grace of God; that no root of bitterness springing up causes trouble, and by it many be defiled" (NASB).

It is important as life-giving leaders that we have trusted pastors or mentors with whom we can share relational issues and disappointments. If we let issues and disappointments sit and fester in our souls, they will be harder to deal with later. Emotional anger not dealt with will lead to sinful bitterness. Remember, no matter our circumstances, the state of our hearts will determine the direction of our lives and our leadership. We need to guard our hearts.

A Life-Giving Leader Knows That Risk Is the Basis of Increase

In Matthew 25, in the parable of the talents, we get a glimpse of how much God values risk-takers. In this parable, the reader finds a master giving talents to his servants and then leaving on a journey. Two of the servants took a risk and invested their talents, while the last servant hid his talent in the ground because he was afraid of the master. When the master came home from his journey, he was pleased with the two servants who took risks. They invested the talents and the master's money increased. Like this master, life-giving leaders value risk-takers. Here is my story of when a ministry leader encouraged me to take a risk.

Julia

Adrenaline was pumping, thoughts were racing, and the time to start the workshop was getting closer. All of the planning that went into this impassioned vision was about to come to fruition in a few short minutes! Watching the clock, I remembered the moment when I presented the idea to my ministry leader. I wanted to create a lab where people could develop mission statements based on their God-given gifts and develop small groups based on their passion—marrying purpose with passion. Encouraging me to take a risk and run with it, my ministry leader gave a resounding, "Absolutely! Go for it!" What began as a God-inspired idea became a reality and the i3 Lab was birthed. "i3" stands for inspire, initiate, and innovate. My ministry leader understood the following things.

- A life-giving leader creates a relational environment that encourages abilities and promotes capacity to change. She invests in her team, allowing them to take risks, make mistakes, learn from those mistakes, and try again.

- A life-giving leader creates a relational environment where there is *no fear of failure* so that team members are not afraid to take risks. My ministry leader cultivated relationships by meeting with each team member on a weekly basis, discussing everything from family life to ministry issues.

A life-giving leader delights in the success of others. When I did my first i3 Lab, I knew my ministry leader supported me and delighted in my success. Even if it wasn't a huge success, I knew that as long as I did my best, my ministry leader would support me. Yes, sometimes support means suggesting ways to do things differently or pointing out mistakes, but I knew deep in my heart that my leader was for me and wanted me to succeed in what God had called me to do.

Small Group Discussion Questions

Characteristics of Life-Giving Leaders

1. Discuss the secret to sustainable joy: a life-giving leader knows that Jesus, not the circumstances of her life, is the One who determines the atmosphere of her soul.

2. Describe a time when you focused on the promises of God rather than your circumstances.

3. Explain the difference between being led by the Holy Spirit and being driven by an unmet need.

4. What are the dangers of a personality-led ministry?

5. When you read the list of intimacy needs, which ones, if any, are you lacking? Identify them and talk with a trusted friend, pastor, mentor, or counselor and determine a healthy strategy to meet these needs.

6. Have you experienced pain as a result of being in leadership, and if so, how did you cope with it?

7. Discuss the parable of the three servants in Matthew 25. How does this parable teach that God values risk-takers?

8. How can you create a relational environment that encourages risk-taking where there is no fear of failure?

Note

[1]David Ferguson and Don McMinn, *Top 10 Intimacy Needs* (Austin: Intimacy Press, 1994), 22–35.

3

Hindrances to Becoming Life-Giving

The majority of my professional life has been spent working as a therapist with at-risk adolescent girls. Whenever I had a new girl assigned to my caseload, I would ask her questions about certain areas or developmental domains of her life so I could assess her well-being. The questions would cover her emotional, physical, relational, spiritual, intellectual, and sexual domains, helping me gather information so I could best address her mental health needs.

One particular question would get an interesting and typically common response. The question was, "Are most of your friends male or female?" The common answer was, "Boys, because girls are too much drama!" They preferred hanging out with boys rather than girls because girls cause trouble.

I cannot tell you how many times I've had adult women say to me, "I don't like women's ministry. I don't like all the drama!" One woman called it "women's misery." Sound familiar? The adolescent girls had the same complaint. Dee Brestin, in her book *The Friendships of Women,* writes: "Little girls, studies show, have a tendency to go straight for the jugular. Girls have a tendency, more than boys, to draw a close intimate circle and leave others out, hurting them deeply. Do we change when we become women? Do we stop throwing darts?"[1]

Sadly, darts of gossip, betrayal, and competition are carried over into church. Bible studies, small groups, women's retreats, and outreaches can become quagmires and cesspools of conflict and marginalization to the point that women leave church and turn away from their faith. So how do we as Christ followers, women called to lead women, change the relational environments in our churches?

As Christ followers, we are called to a higher standard of relational integrity. That standard is love. "This is the message you have heard from the beginning: We should love one another" (1 John 3:11). Our love for one another proves to a lost and dying world that we are his disciples (John 13:35). Why is it so hard for us to love one another, hindering the life-giving, loving nature of Christ? What hinders a woman from being life-giving? To find some of these answers, let us look in 1 Samuel 18 and 19 to learn about Michal, King Saul's second daughter.

First Hindrance: Criticalness

Michal was the daughter of King Saul. She fell in love with David, her father's arch nemesis. First Samuel 18:6–9 gives the reason for Saul's hatred of David.

> When the victorious Israelite army was return-
> ing home after David had killed the Philistine,
> women from all the towns of Israel came out to
> meet King Saul. They sang and danced for joy
> with tambourines and cymbals. This was their
> song: "Saul has killed his thousands, and David
> his ten thousands!" This made Saul very angry.
> "What's this?" he said. "They credit David with
> ten thousands and me with only thousands. Next
> they'll be making him their king!" So from that
> time on Saul kept a jealous eye on David.

King Saul recognized the Spirit of God on David, making Saul afraid of losing his power and position to him. King Saul was jealous of David. It was against this backdrop that Michal fell in love with David and eventually became his wife.

With jealousy fueling his hatred, Saul turned against David and set a plan in place to kill him. Because of Michal's deep love for David, she helped David escape. "So Michal let David down through a window, and he fled and escaped" (1 Sam. 19:12 NIV).

The story continues into 2 Samuel. Over the years, the war between them grew; David grew steadily stronger, but the house of Saul grew weaker. Eventually, Saul died and David was anointed king over all of Israel. "So all the elders of Israel came to the king at Hebron, and King David made a covenant with them at Hebron before the Lord, and they anointed David king over Israel" (2 Sam. 5:3 ESV).

King David's first order of business was to gather thirty thousand chosen men of Israel to bring the ark of God from Baale-judah to its rightful home in Jerusalem. As they were bringing the ark into Jerusalem, a historic and monumental moment in Israel's history, they celebrated before the Lord with music and dancing. Second Samuel 6:14 says, "And David was dancing before the Lord with all his might, and David was wearing a linen ephod" (NASB).

At this moment in the story, Michal, who loved David and had saved him from death, exhibited a critical nature. "Then it happened as the ark of the Lord came into the city of David that Michal the daughter of Saul looked out of the window and saw King David leaping and dancing before the Lord; and *she despised him in her heart*. . . . But when David returned to bless his household, Michal the daughter of Saul came out to meet David and said, 'How the king of Israel distinguished himself today! He uncovered himself today in the eyes of his servants' maids as one of the foolish ones shamelessly uncovers himself!'" (2 Sam. 6:16, 20 NASB; emphasis mine).

In her criticalness, Michal missed a *kairos* moment, the moment that the ark of God was brought into Jerusalem. Embarrassed by David's unabashed display of celebration and worship, she was more concerned with appropriate behavior and keeping up appearances rather than the profound event unfolding before her very eyes. In other words, *she missed it big time.*

Michal went from a loving woman who literally saved David's life to a critical woman full of pride, unable to identify a move of God because she was too concerned with appropriate behavior. Like Michal, it's so easy for us to fall into the trap of criticizing those around us—our friends, families, husbands, church leadership, and on and on. The challenge is to maintain the standard of love set before us by Jesus and not fall into criticalness like Michal, a woman sitting in a window passing judgment on others. Otherwise, we could end up missing what God has for our lives.

Dictionary.com defines *criticalness* as "inclined to find fault or to judge with severity, often too readily."[2] This type of criticalness is different than providing skillful judgment in light of the truth. For example, if one of your leaders was engaged in an adulterous affair, your critical analysis of Scripture against her actions would provide sound judgment in the situation. Providing critical analysis is different in attitude and heart than having a critical nature. Michal had a critical nature toward her husband. Her criticalness smacked of dishonor.

When you venture into the realm of dishonor, you better be prepared to reap what you sow and vice versa. When you honor, you reap the benefits. *The American Dictionary of the English Language* defines honor as "The esteem due or paid to worth; high estimation; a testimony of esteem; any expression of respect or of high estimation by words or actions."[3]

Let's look at Scripture to see the consequences of dishonoring others.

> Do not judge others, and you will not be judged. For you will be treated as you treat others. The standard you use in judging is the standard by which you will be judged. (Matt. 7:1–2)

> You must be compassionate, just as your Father is compassionate. Do not judge others, or it will all come back against you. Forgive others, and you will be forgiven. (Luke 6:36–37)

> Don't speak evil against each other, dear brothers and sisters. If you criticize and judge each other, then you are criticizing and judging God's law. But your job is to obey the law, not to judge whether it applies to you. God alone, who gave the law, is the Judge. He alone has the power to save or to destroy. So what right do you have to judge your neighbor? (James 4:11–12)

So how can we protect ourselves from becoming critical? Choose to honor. Honor is a choice, an attitude, a position of the heart. Honor reaps benefits. Dishonor, criticalness, and judging others reap difficulties and challenges. We are called to honor church leaders, civil leaders, our spouses, and our peers. Here's a peek at a few Scriptures on honor.

Exodus 20:12 says, "Honor your father and mother. Then you will live a long, full life in the land the LORD your God is giving you." 1 Peter 2:17 says, "Respect everyone, and love the family of believers. Fear God, and respect the king." Romans 12:10 says, "Love each other with genuine affection, and take delight in honoring each other." First Timothy 5:17 says, "Elders who do their work well should be respected and paid well, especially those who work hard at both preaching and teaching." Hebrews 13:4 says, "Give honor to marriage, and remain faithful to one another in marriage. God will surely judge people who are immoral and those who commit adultery."

Second Hindrance: Jealousy

Jealousy. It is insidious and flows as an undercurrent in the lives of women everywhere. If left unchecked, jealousy can destroy friendships, families, and lives. The following story is an example of how jealousy wreaked havoc on a family, ravaging their relationships.

Freda

Four of the six chairs around the conference table were filled with a family consisting of a mother, her son, and her two daughters. Missing from the table was their father, who had left them years ago to live with his girlfriend. The family was seeking help because jealousy was tearing them apart. Their journey to this moment started years earlier when their father abandoned the family.

Perhaps you've experienced the pain of having your spouse walk out on you and your family; you know first-hand the profound impact it has on all members of the family. Devastated and emotionally worn out, their mother became depressed and no longer cared for the children. Feeling angry, abandoned, and betrayed by her father, Rayna, the oldest daughter, was left to care for her younger siblings. Her anger and bitterness was so intense toward her father that she severed her relationship with him.

The impact on Freda was very different. Unlike her older sister, Freda felt a special connection with her dad. Although she was angry with her dad for leaving, she was able to forgive him and chose to maintain a relationship with him. Eventually, the father and his girlfriend had two children together, and Freda embraced them as part of the family, while Rayna vehemently stood against her father and rejected his new children.

A root of bitterness, watered by feelings of abandonment and rejection, will wreak havoc on one's soul, and this is what happened to Rayna. She became jealous of Freda's relationship with their dad. Her broken and wounded soul provided fertile ground for jealousy to take root in her heart. And now, Rayna's bitterness and jealousy were tearing this family apart, causing them to seek help through counseling.

Sometimes, when we are reacting out of pain, we are blind to our own sinfulness. This is what happened to Rayna. She blamed their family's issues on Freda. As apparent as it was to her family and me, Rayna stubbornly denied that she was jealous of her sister's relationship with their dad. Freda simply loved her dad and wanted her sister's love and approval as well.

What was I supposed to do? Apart from the love of Christ melting Rayna's heart, there was not much that could be done. Rayna was the linchpin in this scenario. How she responded would determine if the family would reconcile and become healthy. If only she understood that humbling herself, expressing her jealousy, and seeking forgiveness were the keys to reconciliation and healing. Sadly, Rayna left the session with jealousy firmly rooted in her heart, and Freda left still yearning for her older sister's love.

Never before had I seen jealousy so blatantly ruin a relationship as with Freda and Rayna. Working with this family caused me to think about my own character flaws, especially my own struggle with jealousy. I had read the Gospel of Luke several times, but one night as I was reading, the story of the prodigal son changed my paradigm, setting me on a path of healing. Here is my story.

Julia

As a little girl, I struggled with depression and low self-worth. When I became a Christ follower, I took all of my "fleshy junk" to the Lord, asking him to help me overcome these issues. Nothing seemed to work. Somewhere in my background, I had learned to equate love with being good and having the right behavior. I believed that if I was good enough, talented enough, and smart enough, then someone would listen to me and pay attention to me. My family of origin valued performance and productivity over intimate, authentic relationships, causing me to be judgmental and critical of myself and others.

This is not a book about how to overcome your emotional issues. There are several excellent books to cover that topic. However, hurting people hurt people, and when you take a hurting person and mesh that hurt with Christian disciplines, then sometimes a twisted, legalistic view of Christianity emerges, sucking the life out of those around them.

The ability to feel is a gift of God, but when the soul has been wounded through abandonment or abuse, those feelings can be a destructive road to low self-worth with no spiritual direction. Instead of living with the freedom of healthy emotions, we become chained to emotional shipwrecks, rendering us broken and unable to function.

It is interesting that one can provide all the physical needs for a child and totally miss her heart. That is what happened to me. I grew up in a critical environment where performance was valued and intimacy was painful, uncomfortable, and rarely achieved. My soul was wounded, so when I became a Christian, my ability to receive God's love and give love to others was impaired. Finally, after years of walking with this underlying current of sin in my life, my eyes were opened, and my life was "wrecked" by one of Jesus's parables in Luke—the story of the prodigal son. Let's look at this powerful story.

A certain man had two sons. And the younger of them said to his father, "Father, give me the portion of goods that falls to me." So he divided to them his livelihood. And not many days after, the younger son gathered all together, journeyed to a far country, and there wasted his possessions with prodigal living. But when he had spent all, there arose a severe famine in that land and he began to be in want. Then he went and joined himself to a citizen of that country, and he sent him into his fields to feed swine. And he would gladly have filled his stomach with the pods that the swine ate, and no one gave him anything.

But when he came to himself, he said, "How many of my father's hired servants have bread enough and to spare, and I perish with hunger! I will arise and go to my father, and will say to him, 'Father, I have sinned against heaven and before you, and I am no longer worthy to be called your son. Make me like one of your hired servants.'"

And he arose and came to his father. But when he was still a great way off, his father saw him and had compassion, and ran and fell on his neck and kissed him. And the son said to him, "Father, I have sinned against heaven and in your sight, and am no longer worthy to be called your son."

> But the father said to his servants, "Bring out
> the best robe and put it on him, and put a ring
> on his hand and sandals on his feet. And bring
> the fatted calf here and kill it, and let us eat and
> be merry; for this my son was dead and is alive
> again; he was lost and is found." And they began
> to be merry. (Luke 15:11–24 NKJV)

What I love most about this portion of the story is the
father's response. It is a wonderful depiction of God's
heart of love for us. Remember that the father saw his son
when his son "was still a great way off," and he ran to him,
fell on his son's neck, and kissed him. The father did not
heap guilt and condemnation on his son but instructed
his servants to bring out the best robe, put a ring on his
son's hand, and put sandals on his son's feet.

The father could have chosen to handle the situation
differently. He could have rejected his son, yelled at him,
and turned away from him. Instead, he received his son
with arms opened wide, providing us with a beautiful picture of God's love. This is what it means to be life-giving.
The fastest growing churches in America are having the
greatest impact in their communities because they understand this one life-changing, life-giving principle: open
wide your doors to the unsaved, the unchurched, and the
undecided. Impact people's lives with the love of Jesus.

Having read the story of the prodigal son several times,
the second half of this story would always mess with my
"being good" belief system. Again, let's turn to Luke.

Now his older son was in the field, and when he came and approached the house, he heard music and dancing. And he summoned one of the servants and began inquiring what these things might be. And he said to him, "Your brother has come, and your father has killed the fattened calf, because he has received him back safe and sound." But he became angry, and was not willing to go in; and his father came out and began entreating him. But he answered and said to his father, "Look! For so many years I have been serving you, and I have never neglected a command of yours; and yet you have never given me a young goat that I might celebrate with my friends; but when this son of yours came, who has devoured your wealth with prostitutes, you killed the fattened calf for him." And he said to him, "Son, you have always been with me, and all that is mine is yours. But we had to celebrate and rejoice, for this brother of yours was dead and has begun to live, and was lost and has been found." (Luke 15:25–32 NASB)

What? This is the "good" son! I always felt sorry for the "good" son. He stayed home, he worked hard, he did all the right things, but he had one major flaw in his belief system. He did not understand love and grace. If he had been the one to see his brother coming, the story would have turned out much differently. He may have run out to his brother and told him to leave and never come back. How many times have I turned my back on a "prodigal" and, as a result, the prodigal has turned her back on me? Frankly, I would, too.

When I read this, I realized that I was like the second son . . . always trying to be good, trying to do the right thing, and judging others for their poor behavior and poor choices. I remember standing in the church lobby, observing one of our church leaders and thinking to myself, "This guy has such poor social skills. He's rude and cocky." And yet . . . and this began the paradigm shift for me . . . this guy loved Jesus with a passion, and he loved people. God was blessing him, and he was *impacting* people's lives for Jesus. Suddenly, it began to dawn on me that it wasn't his "right behavior" that made him influential. It was his love for Jesus and for people.

After reading the final portion of the parable, I realized that someone could look at me and think I'm a hard-working, loyal, dutiful, and virtuous church member, but a closer inspection would find jealousy, anger, pride, spiritual ambition, and self-righteousness lurking beneath the surface of my soul. I needed an experiential encounter with the Father's love.

I identified with the sins of the older brother of the parable rather than the sins of the younger brother. Like the older brother, I sinned against love, which is diametrically opposed to the gospel; God is love. I was saying and doing all the right things, but inwardly my heart was dark. I cried out to God to help me overcome pride, jealousy, and criticalness. When I realized that I was sinning against love, I began the process of becoming free. Thankfully, this realization broke my heart, and I began to heal spiritually and emotionally. It was for freedom that Christ set me free, and I was determined not to be enslaved in a prison of performance. My transformation came when I realized the truth that God is crazy about me, which enabled me to be kind and open-hearted toward others. This love is the greatest marketing tool for a love-depleted world.

So how did I heal spiritually and emotionally? Let's begin with spiritual health. First, I acknowledged my inability to heal myself. Second Corinthians 12:10 became real to me: "That's why I take pleasure in my weaknesses, and in the insults, hardships, persecutions, and troubles that I suffer for Christ. For when I am weak, then I am strong." I acknowledged my need for him and the work of the Holy Spirit in my life.

Secondly, I believed that what we think determines what we feel which then determines what we do. The model looks like this: Thought – Feeling – Action. For example, if I *thought* about an offense, stewing over how I was hurt or falsely accused, then I found myself *feeling* angry, rejected, and ashamed. That would lead to the *action* of isolating myself from friends, activities, and church.

Self-talk and thought-stopping became valuable tools I used to overcome negative thoughts. When I recalled an offense, I would stop myself from thinking the negative thought and speak truth: "I have forgiven (the person's name here). I am the righteousness of God in Christ Jesus. The Lord will never leave me or forsake me."

Sharon Johnson writes about the origin of negative self-talk in *Therapist's Guide to Clinical Intervention*:

> It starts by a person telling themselves negative things about themselves and their life situation. Not surprisingly, these types of internal messages could start when a person is young because they are unhappy, a negative thing may be repeatedly said to them which becomes part of their identity, they didn't feel like they had control over their life, and/or they have not been taught good coping skills. All of this makes it easier for a person to externalize or blame the way they feel and their responses to some entity outside of themselves and their control instead of taking responsibility for their own feelings and actions.[4]

The way I process life is by talking out what I'm thinking and feeling. So to heal emotionally, I turned to counseling. I also sought out friends who could pray for me and listen to me, but not allow me to stay in a negative place. Journaling is also a valuable tool for healing. Journaling allows you to get your thoughts and feelings out rather than let them fester within, making your internal world fertile ground for bitterness and unforgiveness.

The Third Hindrance: Pride

So what breeds criticalness and jealousy? Pride . . . pride breeds criticalness and jealousy. Thirty scriptures in the Bible warn us of the destructive nature of pride. Pride stands in direct contrast to the love of God and hinders his church from dwelling in unity.

To gain a better understanding of pride, let's look at this analogy. In the middle of the night, you are awakened by water dripping out of your bathroom faucet. Driving you crazy, the noise keeps you awake all night. The first thing you do when you get up in the morning is call a plumber. The plumber comes to your house, pulls out a wrench, and tightens the valve, stopping the water from dripping. The wrench is analogous to pride, and the water is analogous to love.

Pride stops the flow of love. Pride is embedded in insecurity, and I have yet to meet a person who does not have insecurities, perhaps to varying degrees, but all of us have them. That's why it's important to understand the keys to conquering pride so that you can love with the life-giving nature of Christ. Since pride is such a pervasive character issue, we're going to take a more in-depth look in Chapter Four and discover how to be set free from this insidious and dangerous character flaw.

Small Group Discussion Questions

Hindrances to Becoming Life-Giving

1. Did you have positive or negative interactions with girls while growing up?

2. What has been your experience with women's ministry?

3. Have you experienced conflict with other women in a church environment?

4. What ideas do you have to change the relational environments between women within your local church?

5. Explain the difference between critical analysis and a critical nature.

6. Explain how criticalness and judging is dishonoring. Do a Bible study on the consequences of dishonoring others.

7. Is honor a choice or a feeling?

8. How can you honor your leadership as well as those you lead?

9. Have you ever struggled with jealousy, depression, or low self-worth? If so, how have you managed these issues?

10. Let's break down the parable of the prodigal son. What is your reaction to the prodigal son? The father? The older brother? What are your thoughts on grace and love versus law and right behavior as they pertain to this story?

11. How did your father respond to you when you failed or made mistakes?

12. Explain the T-F-A model of behavior. Some people process their thoughts and feelings verbally, some work them out through writing or art, and some just

stuff their thoughts and feelings. How do you process your thoughts and feelings?

Notes

[1] Dee Brestin, *The Friendships of Women* (Wheaton: Victor Books, 1988), 12–13.

[2] "Criticalness," *Dictionary.com*, Random House, accessed January 4, 2015, http://dictionary.reference.com/browse/criticalness.

[3] "Honor," *Webster's Dictionary 1828 – Online Edition*, accessed January 4, 2015, http://webstersdictionary1828.com.

[4] Sharon L. Johnson, *Therapist's Guide to Clinical Intervention* (San Diego: Academic Press, 1997), 189.

4
·········

Keys to Overcoming Hindrances

Walking through the animal shelter, we anxiously looked in each cage for a dog that would be just right for our family. Some of the dogs sat quietly, looking up at us with their sweet, sad eyes. Others jumped up on the cage doors, begging for attention, wanting desperately to be chosen and set free. Just like the cages held the dogs captive, criticalness, jealousy, and pride can hold us captive, hindering us from having a life-giving nature. In this chapter, we're going to look at three keys to overcoming these hindrances: self-love, humility, and forgiveness.

Key Number One: Self-Love

Picture a game of tug-of-war. Pulling one side of the rope is team PRIDE. Pulling the other side is team

SELF-LOVE. In between the two teams is a deep pit filled with insecurities. Team pride keeps trying to pull team self-love into the pit, and team self-love struggles relentlessly to stay out of the pit. Insecurity is the breeding ground for pride. We encase ourselves in pride when we feel less than. We all suffer low self-worth to some degree, and we use pride to cover up the pain. We use pride to puff ourselves up while pulling others down. When we have a healthy sense of love for ourselves, we're able to more fully love others because we love ourselves. Insecurities are left over from our sin nature and work against Christ's commandment to love your neighbor as yourself.

My friends, one of the primary keys to overcoming pride is to love ourselves. It sounds like self-love would evoke pride; however, the type of self-love I'm speaking of is different than an "I'm all that and a bag of chips" type of ego self-love. The type of self-love that I'm writing about is a healthy sense of self which enables us to love others more fully and authentically and to engage the world with confidence.

Self-love is a challenging concept for women to understand and experience. I recently led a group of women church leaders in an activity where I asked each of them to write a love letter to God. In the letter, they were asked to express their love and devotion to the Father as well as explain why they loved him. And then I asked them to write a love letter to themselves, expressing what they loved about themselves and why they loved themselves. Guess which letter was harder to write? If you are a woman reading this, then I'm sure you guessed correctly. Of course the second letter, the love letter to themselves, was more difficult to write. In fact, it was so difficult for some of the women that they chose not to do the exercise. Each woman who wrote a love letter to herself wept as she read her letter to the group.

It is my perspective that many Christian women believe the lie that self-loathing is somehow Christlike and therefore pleasing to God. Self-loathing or self-hatred is an intense dislike for one's self and is usually based in a sense of inadequacy or insecurity. It's a form of false humility. In fact, it is just the opposite of pleasing God. Failing to love ourselves negates all that Jesus did on the cross for us. Because of the redemptive work of the Holy Spirit, believers can experience a solid sense of self and a love for oneself.

Dr. Wilson explains this beautifully in his book *The Grace to Grow*.

> Christianity can make all the difference. Basically this is because of the realistic self-concept that Christianity requires. For the believer, this realistic appraisal of self includes first the understanding that he is a sinner; that is, as a human being he possesses a fallen, unholy spirit, and is therefore naturally separated from God. At the same time, the believer understands that he has been saved from his sinfulness by the redemptive

death of Jesus Christ on the cross, and that he
is empowered to experience wholeness through
the indwelling presence of Christ's Holy Spirit.
The regenerate believer also understands that he
is forever forgiven and unconditionally loved
by God the Father—a Father who values the
personhood of each of His children so much
that He sent His only Son, Jesus, to die for them.
Through Jesus, the believer becomes a "child of
God" in the very truest sense of the phrase.[1]

I love how Dr. Wilson explains that we are children of
God in the truest sense because of his great love for us.
And because of this great love, we can experience wholeness, which includes a healthy sense of self. We find our
value in his love for us. God values each of us so much
that he gave his only Son for you and for me, so that we
could experience his love.

My love for Christ increased as I read and studied
the Bible. We have so many wonderful tools to help us
learn and meditate on Scripture, such as journaling and
even writing them in our mobile devices. I focused on
Scriptures such as 1 John 4:16: "We know how much God
loves us, and we have put our trust in his love. God is
love, and all who live in love live in God, and God lives in
them." And my favorite, Romans 8:31–39:

What shall we say about such wonderful things
as these? If God is for us, who can ever be against
us? Since he did not spare even his own Son

but gave him up for us all, won't he also give us everything else? Who dares accuse us whom God has chosen for his own? No one—for God himself has given us right standing with himself. Who then will condemn us? No one—for Christ Jesus died for us and was raised to life for us, and he is sitting in the place of honor at God's right hand, pleading for us.

Can anything ever separate us from Christ's love? Does it mean he no longer loves us if we have trouble or calamity, or are persecuted, or hungry, or destitute, or in danger, or threatened with death? (As the Scriptures say, "For your sake we are killed every day; we are being slaughtered like sheep.") No, despite all these things, overwhelming victory is ours through Christ, who loved us.

And I am convinced that nothing can ever separate us from God's love. Neither death nor life, neither angels nor demons, neither our fears for today nor our worries about tomorrow—not even the powers of hell can separate us from God's love. No power in the sky above or in the earth below—indeed, nothing in all creation will ever be able to separate us from the love of God that is revealed in Christ Jesus our Lord.

My self-worth improved as I experienced his love through life-giving friendships. I was intentional about seeking out women who were emotionally and spiritually healthy, and developing friendships with them.

As life-giving leaders, we want to encourage women to be involved in relationships where they can experience the love of God. It is true that hurting women hurt other women, but it is also true that we are healed through relationships. That's why life-giving small groups, support groups, mentoring groups, and Bible studies can provide amazing opportunities for healing and growth. The extent to which a woman loves herself is the extent to which she will love others.

Key Number Two: Humility

The second key to overcoming pride is humility. The word humility is derived from the Latin word *humilitas*, which refers to dirt or soil. Dirt can be viewed as filthy and low or as that from which life springs. Genesis 2:7 says, "Then the Lord God formed man of dust from the ground, and breathed into his nostrils the breath of life; and man became a living being" (NASB).

Life-giving leadership is based in humility. Humility is the key to abiding in love. Humility is when we put others before ourselves. We all want to be loved, feel loved, and express love, but we must first understand real love. Love starts with humility. Humility opens the floodgates of water so that his life-giving nature consumes the humble heart.

Let's look at two different examples of humility in the Bible. The first story is found in John 12.

> Jesus, therefore, six days before the Passover,
> came to Bethany where Lazarus was, whom
> Jesus had raised from the dead. So they made
> Him a supper there, and Martha was serving; but
> Lazarus was one of those reclining at the table
> with Him. Mary then took a pound of very costly
> perfume of pure nard and anointed the feet of
> Jesus and wiped His feet with her hair; and the
> house was filled with the fragrance of the per-
> fume. (John 12:1–3 NASB)

Mary committed a deeply humble and loving act by anointing Jesus's feet with expensive perfume.

In fact, we find Jesus exhibiting the same humility in the next chapter of John:

> Jesus, knowing that the Father had given all things
> into His hands, and that He had come forth from
> God and was going back to God, got up from
> supper and laid aside His garments; and taking a
> towel, He girded Himself. Then He poured water
> into the basin, and began to wash the disciples'
> feet, and to wipe them with the towel with which
> He was girded. (John 13:3–5 NASB)

I love Jesus for washing their feet! What a humble act. Jesus, who had everything given to him by God the Father, stooped down to wash the disciples' feet. Jesus was leading his disciples by serving them with humility and love.

God places high value on love and humility. Both love and humility are conditions of the heart, and it is from love and humility that life-giving leaders serve. Jesus said in Mark 10, "[W]hoever wishes to be first among you shall be slave of all. For even the Son of Man did not come to be served, but to serve, and to give His life a ransom for many" (Mark 10:44–45 NASB).

When I was in college, I attended a church where serving others was part of the church culture. One of the pastors was moving across the country to plant another church. He and his wife had three children and a rather large house. His wife broke her ankle and needed help cleaning and packing, so a group of us volunteered to help. One of the girls in our group was asked to clean out the oven. She got angry for having to do such a dirty, menial task. Her attitude was rooted in pride. An older woman helping us said to my friend, and I have never forgotten this: "It is never a waste of time to be humbled." 1 Peter 5:5–7 says, "Clothe your selves with humility toward one another, for GOD IS OPPOSED TO THE PROUD, BUT GIVES GRACE TO THE HUMBLE. Therefore humble yourselves under the mighty hand of God, that He may exalt you at the proper time, casting all your anxiety upon Him, because He cares for you" (NASB).

The Protective Factors of Humility

Having a humble response to others protects our hearts in several ways.

- Humility elevates a relationship so that being right is not the focus, but maintaining the relationship is the priority.
- Humility maintains a pure and innocent heart.
- Humility allows you to give influence away.
- Humility shields you against conflict because it allows you to say four simple, yet powerful, words: "Maybe you are right."
- Humility allows you to acknowledge your own wrongdoings, limitations, and mistakes.
- Humility allows you to receive correction and feedback.
- Humility allows you to learn from your failures.
- Humility allows you to celebrate another's successes.
- Humility allows you to self-reflect on your behavior and words.

A woman who is able to reflect on and analyze her motives is able to adjust her behavior. In other words, if you can listen to your thoughts and words, that self-awareness helps you change. It's been my observation from ministering to and counseling women for several years that not all women are able to objectively analyze their motives. Pride hinders a woman's ability to reflect. However, a humble woman will honestly look at her heart and make adjustments as needed.

We all have blind spots about ourselves. It's important that we give permission to people we respect and trust to speak honestly and frankly with us if they see wrong motives or wrong behaviors based in pride. For example, a wise leader gives permission to her pastor, her husband, and mentors to hold her accountable for her blind spots. Scripture says that dishonor follows pride. Proverbs 11:2 states, "When pride comes, then comes dishonor, but with the humble is wisdom" (NASB). A humble and wise leader examines her motives and allows others to speak into her life when they see that her motives are not pure.

Three Steps to Battling Pride

If you find that you are still battling pride, there are three powerful steps that will help you experience peace and freedom from pride. The steps are repentance, confession, and forgiveness. These three steps are powerful tools that bring life change in the hearts of Christ followers.

Let's begin with the first step, which is repentance. To repent means to change an attitude within your heart. True repentance is initiated by the Holy Spirit, and it serves to restore a right relationship with God. Second Corinthians 7:10 says, "For the kind of sorrow God wants us to experience leads us away from sin and results in salvation. There's no regret for that kind of sorrow. But worldly sorrow, which lacks repentance, results in spiritual death." Unless there is real change in your heart and behavior, then according to this Scripture, it results in spiritual death.

So how do you repent? It is a simple act and yet brings about extraordinary internal changes. All you do is talk to God. Tell him of your struggles with pride. Humbly acknowledge that you want to change and need his help. After repentance comes the second step—confession. Confession means telling God about your heart issues. It's also freeing to confess your sins to a pastor, mentor, or friend. James 5:16 says, "Therefore, confess your sins to one another, and pray for one another so that you may be healed. The effective prayer of a righteous man can accomplish much" (NASB).

I experienced this process during my prayer time when I was convicted by the Holy Spirit of a prideful attitude toward a friend of mine. I knelt beside my bed and repented by asking God to forgive me by the power of the Holy Spirit. I then confessed my prideful attitude to my friend by calling her the next day. I told her what was in my heart and asked her to forgive me. She graciously forgave me. When our conversation ended, I knew my heart was pure and right before the Lord and before my friend, and my soul was at peace. When I got off the phone, I felt as though a weight had been lifted off my shoulders. I felt light and free.

The first step is repentance. The second step is confession, and the third step is the third key: forgiveness.

Key Number Three: Forgiveness

You've heard her . . . a woman who has been deeply hurt by her husband because he had an affair. She talks about it at church, at her job, at the grocery store, and to her hairstylist. Unforgiveness has gotten into her body like water and into her bones like oil. It permeates her life and her relationships, and until she chooses to forgive, she will continue to live in a prison of unforgiveness.

Unforgiveness unleashes a life full of bitterness and a soul that is restless. Sleep becomes elusive. Her soul becomes dark and depressed. She never again experiences true joy or peace until she is able to cross over into the "sweet spot" full of mercy and grace known as forgiveness.

Life-giving leaders choose forgiveness. When a woman sows unforgiveness, she is sowing to her own flesh, but when she sows forgiveness, she is sowing to the Spirit. Perhaps that's why Paul writes in 1 Corinthians 13:5, "Love . . . keeps no records of wrongs" (NIV). Remember, the fruit of the Spirit is love, joy, peace, patience, kindness, goodness, faithfulness, gentleness, and self-control. Notice that unforgiveness is *not* on the list.

Forgiveness is a choice, a powerful choice that breaks chains within us. Bonnie is a life-giving leader whose leadership and influence impact the local church where she serves. Birthed out of a painful accident, Bonnie's story of forgiveness illustrates the life change that occurs when we choose to forgive. She shared this account with me during a personal interview.

Bonnie

On April 2, 2002, my life was changed forever. I got a phone call from my dad. He was calling from the hospital with words I never thought I would hear. My seventeen-year-old sister, Stacy, was in the ICU, and my mother had died. I was alone when I got the news. How could this have happened?

Stacy was in a coma fighting for her life. Her head was fractured on every side, and she had bleeding and swelling in her brain. She had a broken arm and collarbone among other injuries. The area of her brain affected was speech and memory. Doctors anticipated that she would need a lengthy stay in a rehab hospital if she came out of the coma. Stacy continued to sleep while we had my mother's funeral. At one point, her head swelled so badly she was hardly recognizable.

Meanwhile, the man who caused the crash was prosecuted by the state for negligent homicide. I started to look for revenge against this man who had caused the terrible accident which had stolen so much from me. I was hurt. I was angry. I was confused.

But then ten days after the accident, Stacy woke up. The first thing she did was attempt to call our mother on the hospital telephone. My father and a trauma counselor told her that mom had died. On Mother's Day, she watched the funeral we had recorded for her. The one ray of light in the midst of this tragedy was the miracle God was doing with Stacy.

In the beginning, the doctors gave her a 75 percent chance of having some type of brain damage. They also said she would likely have to learn to cope with a speech impediment. But after only one day in the rehab hospital, it was evident that her speech and mental capabilities were rapidly improving. She was discharged. The doctors called her the Miracle Girl! A month to the day after the accident, Stacy was back in school and got a 99 and 100 on two pop quizzes.

I began a two-year journey that brought me to the point of forgiveness. In the beginning of this process, I couldn't fathom forgiving the man who had killed my mother. I would drive by his street and think of ways I could get back at him. Jesus commands us to forgive, but I just wasn't ready, so I got involved in the court process. But then I learned that I couldn't find justice in the justice system. Of course, what I was really looking for was revenge. God showed me that my heart attitude had to be right and not accusatory. After a long battle within myself, I decided to let God be the ultimate judge. If you seek revenge in your heart, it will only turn into bitterness and hate and thwart the calling of God on your life and your relationship with him and others.

I realized I had to let it go. I had to get rid of the blame and the hate. To live with a pure conscience was of greater value to me than trying to avenge my mother's death. So I chose to forgive him. My heart started to soften when I made the conscious decision to forgive. I was still hurting, but the anger and confusion began to fade.

Even though the process of forgiveness had started, something was holding it back. I felt like I had to tell this man that I forgave him. I did not want to! In fact, this was the last thing I ever wanted to do. At one of the final court hearings, we were in a room with him and I talked to him and his wife. I held his hand and told him "I forgive you." It was by far the hardest thing to do, but from that point on, my heart was free. I can't begin to describe how wonderful it is to live with a free heart—free of anger, hurt, bitterness, revenge, and hatred. When I was asked to share this testimony of forgiveness, I realized that I did not even remember the man's name.[2]

If Bonnie had chosen not to forgive the man who killed her mother, her life would be stained with anger and bitterness, derailing her life to the point that she would be ineffective in her ministry to women. Psalm 109:17–18 says, "He also loved cursing, so it came to him; and he did not delight in blessing, so it was far from him. But he clothed himself with cursing as with his garment, and it entered into his body like water and like oil into his bones" (NASB). Instead, Bonnie is married with two smart, lovely daughters, and she and her husband are passionate about sharing the transforming love of Jesus Christ. And her sister is now married and she too has a little girl.

Mastering the art of forgiveness is not an easy journey for any of us. Yet the most valuable, humbling, stretching experiences as Christ followers and leaders occur during pain and conflict. Bonnie knew that if she didn't forgive this man, she would be stuck in a prison of bitterness, hate, and unforgiveness. She had a choice to make. She could stay stuck in a quagmire of mud, or she could break free and choose to forgive. She chose forgiveness.

Many of us will never experience the pain and loss that Bonnie experienced; however, as leaders, we will inevitably offend someone or someone will offend and hurt us. Relational conflict is part of the leadership package, especially when we make difficult decisions that not everyone we lead will understand or agree with. Challenges in ministry provide the greatest opportunities for spiritual growth, which in turn enrich our leadership.

It's also very important to let go and move forward. One important step to moving forward is viewing the person who has hurt you as a gift. Seeing this person as a gift instead of an adversary allows us to examine our own part of the conflict, perhaps revealing character flaws that need to be dealt with. It's important to remember that none of us is perfect and we all make mistakes. Remember, there is no condemnation for those of us who are in Christ Jesus. This frees us to receive grace, forgive ourselves, and move forward.

My most valuable, humbling, stretching experience as a Christ follower and leader occurred during a relational conflict with another woman leader. The lessons I learned from confrontation are priceless. Here is my story.

Julia

My stomach was in knots, and I was holding back waves of nausea. One would think I was battling a virus. Not so. In my mind, it was something far worse: confrontation. My body was reacting to the emotional turmoil I was experiencing as I sat across the conference table from another woman in leadership. And it was not just the two of us. The conflict had escalated to the point where our husbands and pastors were involved. Uncomfortable, awkward, painful—but the leadership lessons I gleaned that day were invaluable.

Inherent in leadership is the probability that you are going to make someone angry or offend someone, resulting in confrontation. Sitting at the conference table, I knew the trajectory of this conversation was going to be determined by my willingness to humble myself. But how could I humble myself when I felt like jumping across the table and punching her lights out? Here are a few tips I used to prepare my heart and mind.

I reminded myself that this woman was not my enemy. Ephesians 6:12 reminds us, "For we are not fighting against flesh-and-blood enemies, but against evil rulers and authorities of the unseen world, against mighty powers in this dark world, and against evil spirits in the heavenly places."

I prayed that God would bless her family, her work, her ministry. Matthew 5:43–48 says, "You have heard the law that says, 'Love your neighbor' and hate your enemy. But I say, love your enemies! Pray for those who persecute you! In that way, you will be acting as true children of your Father in heaven. For he gives his sunlight to both the evil and the good, and he sends rain on the just and the unjust alike. If you love only those who love you, what reward is there for that? Even corrupt tax collectors do that much. If you are kind only to your friends, how are you different from anyone else? Even pagans do that. But you are to be perfect, even as your Father in heaven is perfect." After reading this, I knew that I would be no different than a nonbeliever if I didn't choose to love this woman. Love trumps everything.

I knew that if I didn't forgive her, I would be stuck in a prison of bitterness and unforgiveness. I wanted to go into the meeting with a heart ready to seek understanding and restore our relationship. The goal was not for us to be best friends, but to have mutual respect and understanding so that we could work together. Here are a few steps I used to aid the process of forgiving.

- I wrote Scriptures about forgiveness on index cards and kept them in strategic places where I would easily see them: my office desk, my car, my bathroom mirror.
- I read books on forgiveness.
- I reminded myself that forgiveness is a choice, not a feeling. I knew I needed to choose forgiveness.
- Seeing this leader as a gift instead of an adversary allowed me to examine my heart, revealing character flaws that needed to be dealt with.
- I confessed my anger and unforgiveness to my pastor and gave him permission to address blind spots in my character. I asked him to hold me accountable for my attitude.

- I remembered that there is no condemnation for those of us who are in Christ Jesus, which freed me to receive grace, forgive myself, and move forward.

Prior to this situation, I didn't realize how much pride, insecurity, and jealousy was lurking in the recesses of my soul. This relational fracture forced me to look deeply at my character and examine my internal life. It was a golden opportunity to examine my own motives and attitudes and take responsibility for my part in the relational conflict.

Since that uncomfortable meeting in that conference room, my relationship with this woman is peaceful. I do occasionally have a negative internal reaction to her, but in those moments, I remember that forgiveness and love are choices, and I choose to love and honor her. I have had more challenging relational situations since then, giving me more opportunities to humble myself, choose forgiveness, and move forward.

The lessons I gleaned from confrontation strengthened my leadership. These lessons include empathizing and helping other women through relational difficulties; identifying and addressing internal weaknesses in myself before they become an issue; highlighting the principles of unity, honor, and respect with my leaders; being quick to forgive and slow to offend; and giving people the benefit of the doubt.

A beautiful result of these lessons has been a more intimate love relationship with the Lord. Becoming more aware of my need for him and his unconditional love, mercy, and grace in spite of my soul's imperfections has deepened my relationship with him, causing me to more fully love those I serve. Being able to forgive enabled me to calm my emotions and have a satisfying life full of love and joy with him and with others. Now, let's turn to the next chapter where we'll explore life-giving strategies for successful leadership.

Small Group Discussion Questions

Keys to Overcoming Hindrances

1. Write a love letter to the Lord. How was this experience?

2. Now write a love letter to yourself. How was this experience compared to writing a love letter to the Lord?

3. On a scale of 1 to 10, with 10 being the highest and 1 being the lowest, rate how much you love yourself.

4. Discuss your thoughts about this statement: "The extent to which a woman loves herself is the extent to which she will love others."

5. Discuss healthy, life-giving relationships that have exemplified the loving nature of God for you.

6. Discuss your thoughts about this statement: "It is never a waste of time to be humbled."

7. As a leader, have you given key people in your life permission to hold you accountable for your blind spots?

8. Why are repentance, confession, and forgiveness powerful steps in overcoming criticalness and jealousy?

9. Discuss your thoughts on this statement: "When a woman sows unforgiveness, she is sowing to her flesh,

but when she sows forgiveness, she is sowing to the Spirit."

10. Describe a time when you had to choose to forgive.

11. Have you ever had to confront someone? What was this experience like for you?

12. Have you ever been confronted, and if so, how did you respond?

Notes

[1] William P. Wilson, *The Grace to Grow* (Waco: Word Books, 1984), 113.

[2] Bonnie McKinley, "I Chose to Forgive," email message to author, December 2, 2012.

5

Strategies of Life-Giving Leaders

I had recently given birth to our third baby, a sweet, precious baby girl. After two rambunctious boys, we were more than delighted to have some pink around our house. Like all new mothers, I was exhausted. I spent little time fixing my hair, wearing makeup, or wearing anything other than sweats or jeans. The focus of my life was caring for my three little ones. My world consisted of the grocery store, doctor's appointments, hanging out with friends with kids the same age as mine, and attending church. It was during this backdrop that I developed one of the most meaningful friendships I've ever experienced.

Have you ever had someone come into your life at just the right time, and you knew this person was a direct gift from God? Linda was one such gift. Linda was maybe fifteen years older than I was. We went to the same church. I don't remember much about the first time we met; I don't even remember the content of our conversations. I just remember how she made me feel. Whenever she saw me, she would greet me with a big hug and say, "There's that beautiful, talented Julia Mateer!" Now, as I mentioned, I was in a season of life when being attractive was not a priority, and in terms of being talented . . . well, let's just say my talents consisted of wrangling two wild boys from getting into things that were off-limits. Nevertheless, that's how she would greet me.

Eventually, Linda began to call and ask how my day was going. We started meeting every two weeks for lunch, and during our lunches, she asked me about my life and my dreams. She listened as I shared my struggles, and she purposed to pray for me.

Linda saw potential in me. She made me feel important, valued, and confident. A year after we met, she and her husband relocated. I will always be grateful for Linda. I don't think she knew just how much our time together meant or the positive impact her friendship had on me. It was such a beautiful gift from the Father.

Believing in another woman and helping to develop her potential is one of the greatest opportunities for a life-giving leader. In this chapter, we are going to look at life-giving strategies to help us cultivate the potential within the women we serve. Let's begin with words. A life-giving leader knows the power of her words.

Strategy Number One: Bless with Words

Wracked with insecurities and self-doubt, a young woman found herself in my office seeking counseling. Quietly crying, she recounted growing up with emotionally distant parents. She could not recall one encouraging word or one act of support from her mom or dad. On the contrary, her memories were full of criticism, belittling statements, and verbal abuse. Her heart was encased in a prison of self-doubt and insecurity. If only her parents knew the havoc they inflicted on their daughter's soul. If only they had believed in her and encouraged her. They could have unlocked her potential, helping her to become confident and secure. Instead, their daughter was broken and deeply wounded.

The most *powerful* leadership tool we have is our words. James 3:6 says that the tongue sets the course of life on fire. The very existence of one's life is set into motion by words. This young woman had not reached her full potential because her potential had not been "spoken to" by the people who mattered most—her parents. The message conveyed to their daughter was, "You can't do anything right. You are a bother to us. Why did we have you? You are one big mistake. You will never amount to anything." The direction of her life would've been much different if she'd heard encouragement like, "You are awesome! What a blessing you are to us. We are so proud of you. You can do all things through Christ who strengthens you. We are 100 percent for you."

During our time together, I spoke words of encouragement to her, focusing on her strengths and potential. I helped her establish her identity in Christ by having her focus on the transformative power of Scripture. Hebrews 4:12 says, "For the word of God is alive and powerful. It is sharper than the sharpest two-edged sword, cutting between soul and spirit, between joint and marrow. It exposes our innermost thoughts and desires." The Word of God is alive, and as my client meditated on and memorized Scripture, she began to see herself as Christ sees her, as Christ sees all of us: valuable, loved, and cherished.

What a powerful opportunity we have as life-giving leaders to create an atmosphere of blessing with our words, whether in our homes with our families, in businesses with our employees, or in churches with fellow church members. Kevin Harney writes in his book *Leadership from the Inside Out*, "Churches where words of kindness and encouragement are plentiful have the aroma of life. I have walked into congregations and felt the health and joy that exist because of their culture of blessing. The opposite is true. Congregations and staffs that are filled with criticism, backbiting, and gossip have the stench of death."[1]

Words that do not shine the light of Christ increase the darkness. I have been a part of organizations where the women in leadership used cuss words as every part of the English language: verbs, nouns, adverbs, adjectives creating a critical and angry atmosphere and filling the air with the "stench of death." Sadly, these women missed opportunities to bless and empower their staffs. Ephesians 4:29 says, "Let no unwholesome word proceed from your mouth, but only such a word as is good for edification according to the need of the moment, so that it will give grace to those who hear" (NASB).

A life-giving leader knows the importance of setting a guard over her mouth and watching the door of her lips (Ps. 141:3), choosing words that intentionally create an affirming environment. Instead of a culture of critical-ness and negativity, a life-giving leader blesses with her words. Make your words life-giving, full of mercy and grace. Here are a few ideas to bless and affirm the people in your sphere of responsibility.

- Praise your leaders in front of others
- Write shout-outs on social media
- Put pictures of team meetings on social media
- Deliver handwritten notes of appreciation
- Give gifts specific and unique to each individual

Strategy Number Two: Value Your Team

Whether by shepherding, mentoring, or managing, a life-giving leader knows how to value the women she leads, and she never gives up on any member of her team. Jesus *never* gave up on anyone. He gave every chance to those who made mistakes and failed, betrayed, and denied him. Look how he stood by Judas. Look how he stood by Peter. Look at how he stands by you and me. He will never forsake us or leave us. Nothing can separate us from his love. Kristin is one such leader who knows how to value her team.

Kristin

Kristin is the Director of Creative Development at one of the fastest growing churches in America. Because of her life-giving leadership, her talented staff produces some of the best visuals in the country at their weekend services. She believes that church should be the safest place for people to make mistakes. "After all," Kristen says, "God is the God of infinite chances." And because she creates a safe and life-giving environment for her team, they create mind-blowing, creative work that could not come about if her team members were afraid to use their imaginations and take risks.

Kristin creates a safe environment by valuing her team. She believes that in order to keep members of her team, they must know they are valued. "Bring them their favorite coffee, a gift card; find out their love language. Value their strengths and know and cover their weaknesses. Value your team like you value a new pair of jeans!"[2]

Strategy Number Three: Connect

A life-giving leader connects with others like a cord plugging into an electrical outlet, bringing light to people's hearts and minds. When women connect with women through the cords of Scripture, prayer, or words of wisdom, life-giving relationships form, and lives are changed for eternity. Jesus came to earth for us. He lived and died for you and me. We matter to him. If you and I matter to him, then people need to matter to us. We were designed to connect. Connecting is part of our spiritual DNA. As we plug into God, we experience true life, and as we connect with others, that life is expressed through the love we have for one another.

Connecting with others is a have-to for a life-giving leader. Jesus, the ultimate connector, said, "This is My commandment, that you love one another, just as I have loved you. Greater love has no one than this, that one lay down his life for his friends" (John 15:12–13 NASB). We are *commanded* to love each other.

Michelle

Michelle, a successful CPA with three children and a leader in her church, was driving home from the office when she got a call on her cell. Julie, one of her small group leaders, had been in a car accident and rushed to the hospital. Immediately, Michelle kicked into high gear! She went straight home, got her children settled, and lined up meals for Julie. As soon as her husband got home from work, Michelle went to the hospital to visit and pray with her.

Making calls, lining up meals, and rushing to the hospital were not in Michelle's plans after a long day at the office. Like most working moms, she would rather have stayed at home, made dinner, and spent time with her family, but Michelle knows the importance of being available to connect with the women she leads.

Shawna

Life-giving connectors engage women on an emotional level by extending love, kindness, and encouragement. Shawna is a natural connector. After a church service, Shawna can be found holding and praying with a crying woman or encouraging a woman by taking her out for coffee. She may send her a text or connect with her on Facebook.

Shelly

Shelly Juskiewicz, Pastor to Women at Mariners Church in Irvine, California, connected with women in her community who would never come through church doors by creating the Diva Bus Tour. The Diva Bus took women from the church out into the community to connect with women in need. They filled the bus with diapers and food and advertised on Craigslist that they would be in the area with free lunch and diapers. They met the practical needs of the women, developed relationships, and had critical conversations that would never have taken place inside the church walls. Shelly and the women on the Diva Bus Tour made themselves available, made connections, and were the hands and feet of Jesus.

Strategy Number Four: Listen

Life-giving leaders pause long enough to hear someone's story, to hear beyond the words, and to hear what is in the heart, making the person feel valued because she has been heard. The women we lead need to know that they have our full attention. What does this look like? Make eye contact and be slow to speak, keeping your eyes on the person to whom you are speaking. Do not let your gaze wander. Occasionally repeat what you have heard to assure the speaker that you understand her, and keep your mind focused on what is being said and not on your grocery list or what you are going to say next.

The majority of communication is listening, not speaking. The word *listen* occurs more than three hundred times in the Bible. The Book of Proverbs says, "To answer before listening—that is folly and shame" (Prov. 18:13 NIV). James reminds us, "Everyone should be quick to listen, slow to speak and slow to become angry" (James 1:19 NIV). A life-giving leader shows that she values the person by listening . . . really listening to what is in the heart, not just the words. But what happens when the majority of communication is speaking and *not* listening? Let's find out.

At 11:00 A.M. and already 84 degrees, it was a hot Florida morning as I drove with my twelve-year-old daughter, Caroline, to meet friends for brunch. To say that I dreaded this brunch was an understatement. I dreaded it because one of the women liked to talk . . . constantly . . . about herself . . . with no awareness that there were other women at the table who might want to say something . . . anything. It was a miserable experience. I sat there smiling, nodding my head, and thinking to myself that I would *never* waste another Saturday morning listening to this woman go on and on.

As soon as brunch was over, we said our good-byes, and Caroline and I got into our car. Turning to me, she said, "Mommy, that woman is a selfish listener." I asked her what she meant by "selfish listener," and she said, "A selfish listener is someone that only talks about herself and doesn't include anyone else in the conversation." Needless to say, I was pretty impressed with my daughter's astute observation, and I thoroughly agreed with her.

Strategy Number Five: Boss Your Brain

A successful life-giving leader must first know how to lead herself before she can lead others. This is done by monitoring your thoughts; you lead yourself by monitoring your thoughts and being aware of your inner life. Jesus was keenly aware of this principle. In Mark 7:14–15, Jesus is speaking to a crowd, and he says, "Listen to Me, all of you, and understand: there is nothing outside the man which can defile him if it goes into him; but the things which proceed out of the man are what defile the man" (NASB). The word *defile* is not a word we hear in our culture today, but according to thefreedictionary.com, it means "to make filthy or dirty; to pollute; to debase the pureness or excellence of; to corrupt."[3]

Your thought life determines the direction of your life. Proverbs 23:7 says, "For as he thinks within himself, so he is" (NASB). As a therapist, one of the first principles I learned is that what you think determines what you feel, which determines what you do. The model looks like this: T–F–A. What you think becomes your reality. What you think determines what you feel, which determines your actions: think – feel – actions. Thoughts lead to feelings which lead to actions, making it vital to monitor your thought life.

However, here is a priceless truth: thoughts are just thoughts. They have no impact on you unless you allow them. Remember, our souls consist of our minds, wills, and emotions. If we partner with thoughts that are lies, the thoughts will negatively impact us. For example, maybe you made a mistake on your budget and over-drew your account. You find yourself thinking, "I'm a real screwup when it comes to my finances. I must be so stupid." These negative thoughts begin to make you feel negatively about yourself, which leads you to think you're incapable of taking care of your finances. What we think determines what we feel, which determines our behavior. That's why Scripture encourages us to take every thought captive to the obedience of Christ (2 Cor. 10:5).

I love the phrase "boss your brain." When my oldest son was young, he was diagnosed with ADHD. One of the most important strategies he learned was to filter his thoughts by bossing his brain. I have used this phrase both as a therapist with my clients and with my own children.

For example, Amy struggled with her weight. Her weight was in the obese range. As a teenager, she was a victim of sexual abuse. She blamed herself, keeping the assault a secret for years. Her negative thoughts produced feelings of guilt, shame, anger, and worthlessness. Her feelings led her to comfort herself with food, often eating whole pies and bags of cookies. Her negative thoughts led to negative feelings, which led to negative actions. The scriptural basis is found in Proverbs 23:7: "For as he thinks within himself, so he is" (NASB).

Often I hear women speak as if they have minimal input or control in determining their lives or the choices they make. I'll hear something like this: "Whatever happens is the way it's supposed to be." That somehow life just happens to us and we have no control. Somewhere in their theological upbringing, they bought into the lie that their lives are dictated by fate. Not true. God gave us the ability to think and make wise choices. Let's look at Scripture to find God's perspective on our ability to think and choose for ourselves.

According to 2 Timothy 1:7, we're created with the ability to discipline ourselves. "For God has not given us a spirit of fear and timidity, but of power, love, and self-discipline." Second Timothy 2:15 says, "Work hard so you can present yourself to God and receive his approval. Be a good worker, one who does not need to be ashamed and who correctly explains the word of truth." James 1:5 says we can ask for wisdom. "If you need wisdom, ask our generous God, AND HE will give it to you. He will not rebuke you for asking."

Life-giving thoughts lead to life-giving change. Let's look at how this truth transformed Connie's life.

Connie

Connie's father was never a part of her life, and her mom lost custody not only of Connie but of all her children when she was sent to prison for selling drugs. Having spent most of her childhood in and out of foster homes, Connie struggled with feelings of low self-worth, mistrust, shame, and rejection. As a teen, Connie sought attention and love from boys, resulting in a pregnancy at sixteen. She made the painful yet brave decision to give the baby up for adoption.

By the age of thirty, Connie had been married and divorced twice. She was tired of cycling through unhealthy and unsuccessful relationships. Lonely and discouraged, Connie wanted to change, but in order to do so, she knew she needed help. She shared with her girlfriend how she was feeling, and her girlfriend invited her to church.

The next Sunday, Connie went to church for the first time. By the end of the service, Connie had become a Christ follower. For the first time in her life, she heard about God's love. He loved her even if she had made multiple mistakes, multiple bad choices. It didn't matter. He loved her. That morning, her heart grabbed hold of the truth and did not let it go. This beautiful, transformative truth captivated her, and she knew she had found the love she had always been seeking.

Determined to view her life through the lens of biblical truth rather than from a wounded, twisted perspective,

Connie sought counseling from a Christian counselor. The first several sessions focused on healing the pain from Connie's childhood. All of the negative thoughts about herself had caused her to feel negatively about herself, which drove her to make decisions that caused even more pain. It was during this point in Connie's healing that her counselor shared the importance of renewing her mind by monitoring her thoughts. If she thought of herself as worthless, she would throw away that thought and meditate on a Scripture about the truth of who she was in Christ: "I am the righteousness of God in Christ Jesus." Bossing her brain, Connie would meditate on the truth of how Jesus thought of her.

As Connie's thought life was rewired, she began to feel better about herself, to actually love herself. She exemplified Isaiah 61:3, "To all who mourn in Israel, he will give a crown of beauty for ashes, a joyous blessing instead of mourning, festive praise instead of despair. In their righteousness, they will be like great oaks that the LORD has planted for his own glory." Connie wanted to share her newfound freedom with other women who were captives of emotional trauma, and she became a vital, life-giving volunteer counselor at her church.

Strategy Number Six: Manage Your Emotions

As a therapist and women's pastor, I know the importance of keeping our emotional world healthy. But how do we do this? How does a life-giving woman manage her emotions? Does God even care about this area of a woman's life? He absolutely cares about this area of your life. The Bible says that your finances and health will prosper as your soul prospers (3 John 1:2). Remember that your soul is made up of your mind (thoughts), will, and emotions. So if your soul is prospering, which includes your mind, will, and emotions, than everything else will prosper, too.

Your internal world of the soul impacts your external world. For example, if I am struggling with anger, anxiety, or frustration, I am much more likely to yell at my kids or be impatient with the store clerk. On the contrary, if I've had a great night's sleep, I'm relaxed, and I feel content, then I'm going to exude an overall sense of well-being whether I'm at the office, at church, with my family, at the grocery store, or wherever my day takes me.

The key to managing your emotions is to acknowledge your real emotions. Many Christian women consider it a sin to feel emotions such as anger, sadness, disappointment, discouragement, and fear. Often, women will stuff these emotions, thinking it is a sin to feel them. Some women fear being judged and condemned as having a lack of faith if they express these emotions.

The problem with stuffing emotions is that depression, criticalness, and bitterness will surface and override life-giving joy and love. In order to keep your internal world healthy, it is imperative to have safe people in your life with whom you can openly and honestly share your feelings. You want to choose wise people who will not let you sit in your negative emotions but will spur you on and forward, people who will give you a hand out of your emotional pit and not get down in the pit with you and have an emotional pity party.

Dana

Dana is a great example of a woman who manages her emotions through difficult situations. Dana directs a non-profit organization that cares for at-risk families. During the first few weeks as director, she realized one particular staff member was underperforming and needed to be removed. Dana had to make a tough decision to fire the staff member.

In making this decision, Dana experienced internal conflict, even though she was confident it was the right decision for the company and ultimately for the staff member as well. Women in leadership are called upon to make difficult decisions. One of the most difficult decisions is removing someone from his or her position, whether the person is paid or a volunteer.

Sally

Internal discomfort is a normal part of making difficult decisions. Remember that feelings are not necessarily a call to action. For example, Sally has worked with poor migrant families in her community for several years. In the early days of her ministry, she found a young pregnant woman with four children living in a duplex with no beds, no appliances, and no air conditioning; the husband was in jail.

Moved by compassion, Sally delivered beds, appliances, and an air conditioner to her home. Weeks later, she went to check on this family and found the beds assembled and in use, but the air conditioner and the appliances were sitting where she had left them. The young mother did not have anyone to install the air conditioner, nor did she have the money to pay the electric bill for the appliances. What Sally perceived as a blessing for this family was in fact a burden to them. She learned a valuable leadership lesson that morning: feelings are not necessarily a call to action. Pursuing a strategy to alleviate emotional discomfort is not always the best path for a leader or those that she serves.

The following are six steps for healthy and productive decision-making:

- Pray and ask God for wisdom. James 1:5 says, "But if any of you lacks wisdom, let him ask of God, who gives to all generously and without reproach, and it will be given to him" (NASB).
- Identify the objective and outcomes; think through the impact of your decision.
- Take emotions out of the decision-making process by doing your homework and gathering pertinent facts.
- Brainstorm with a group of respected and trusted friends, including your spiritual authority. Proverbs 15:22 says, "Without consultation, plans

are frustrated, but with many counselors they succeed" (NASB).

- List and prioritize the pros and cons of your
decision. Lead with your thoughts and not your
emotions.
- Finally, make a decision, move forward with confidence, and then let it go.[4]

Empowering Women through Small Groups

A small group is a powerful vehicle by which we can utilize these valuable strategies to help cultivate the potential not only within ourselves but also with the women
we serve.

Sitting in my living room was a group of thirty
women gathered for the first week in a twelve-week
small group semester to study Lisa Bevere's book, *Lioness
Arising*. Some women sat pensively waiting for the group
to officially begin, while others buzzed about the room
introducing themselves and connecting. While the group
gathered to read, learn, and study the book, something
deeper happened . . . something of greater consequence
. . . something more meaningful: women's lives were
changed. During the twelve-week small group, friendships were birthed, women became more fully devoted
followers of Christ, and some experienced positive relationships with other women for the first time.

We know that life change happens in the context of
relationships. Look at Jesus. Everything he did was in the
context of relationship. He died and was resurrected for

us . . . relationship. He discipled twelve men . . . relationship. When he ascended to sit at the right hand of the Father, he left the Holy Spirit as our Helper . . . relationship. The local church is all about relationship.

When I think of my own spiritual growth, I think of the people who have invested in my life by praying, encouraging, supporting, and challenging me. I learned how to pray by listening to my college roommate pray. I learned how to worship by watching the people in my local church. I learned how to study and read my Bible by attending a Bible study small group. I learned how to be a wife, a mother, a friend, and a leader through relationships.

Life change happens in and through relationships, and small groups are a perfect format to create the types of life-giving environments where women can grow in their relationship with others and with God. Small groups empower women to lead in the local church, and they provide opportunities for women to implement the strategies mentioned in this chapter.

There are a variety of small group models implemented by churches of different sizes. The two most popular models are the closed group model and the free-market model.

Briefly, the closed group model has the following parameters:

- The topic is determined by church leadership.
- Once a certain number of people are in the group, the group closes.

- There is a beginning and an end to the group.

The free-market model has the following parameters:

- Topic is determined by the leader of the group.
- The group usually stays open so people can join the group at any time.
- There is a beginning and an end to the group.

Both of these models provide great opportunities to develop healthy, life-giving community between group members. When you lead a small group, you have the opportunity to identify other leaders and call forth their potential. You get to create life-giving atmospheres within your group where women feel loved, safe, and encouraged. You get to stretch your leadership muscles and utilize your leadership strategies: connecting women with women, listening to the women in your group, using the power of your words to call forth potential, valuing the women in your group, and encouraging the women you lead as well as yourself to boss your brain and manage your emotions.

The small group structure that I am most familiar with is the free-market model. My local church where I serve as Director of Small Groups has several thousand members. Our pastoral staff cannot effectively shepherd that many people. So small groups are where our people are shepherded. Here's what the leadership structure looks like:

- The **small group leader** takes care of the women in her group. For example, if a woman in her group were to have a baby, then the leader would coordinate meals for her family. The small group leader prays for and encourages the women in her group.
- The **small group coach** shepherds three to five small group leaders.
- The **lead coach** shepherds three to five coaches and is responsible for reproducing groups.
- The **director of women's small groups** is responsible for the entire category of women's small groups.

This small group structure affords women an opportunity to fulfill their God-given potential and impact women with the gospel of Jesus through groups. Here is a beautiful testimony from Gloria, a women's small group leader, who has found fulfillment in leading groups.

Gloria

Personally, I have changed completely because of small groups. I had not felt comfortable with women since my childhood. I had issues with women, but through small groups, I have found that we are the greatest influence to encourage each other. I kept reading Scripture that talked about fellowship being important and how we lean on each other for support and confess our sins to each other that we may be healed. Now I live those Scriptures through small groups with wonderful godly women who love the Lord as I do and can relate to the ups and downs of life together. I believe that Christ saves us but small groups grow us in the love of Christ.[4]

Small Group Discussion Questions

Strategies for Life-Giving Leaders

1. Discuss a time when someone believed in you and helped you reach your full potential. Have you done this for someone else, and if so, what was it like for you and for that person?

2. Brainstorm and develop some "out of the box" ideas for connecting with women in your community.

3. How are you as a listener? Are you a selfish listener? Next time you are conversing, be aware of your eye contact and how much you're allowing the other person to speak.

4. Discuss how thoughts determine the trajectory of your life. What are strategies you can use to boss your brain?

5. Do you agree or disagree that feelings are not necessarily a call to action? Discuss a time when you made a decision driven by an emotional response. What was the outcome?

6. Do you agree that the most powerful leadership tool is our words? If so, why? If not, what do you think is the most powerful leadership tool?

7. What does it mean to create an atmosphere of blessing with our words? How would you rate yourself in this area of your leadership?

8. How can you affirm the people you lead?

9. Have you ever been involved in a small group? If so, describe your experience.

10. What type of small group model fits in the church you attend?

11. What do you think makes a group successful?

Notes

[1] Kevin Harney, *Leadership from the Inside Out* (Grand Rapids, MI: Zondervan, 2007), 101.

[2] Kristin Becnel, "Valuing Your Team," personal interview, Bradenton, FL, October 23, 2010.

[3] "Defile," *thefreedictionary.com*, Farlex, accessed January 4, 2015, www.thefreedictionary.com/defile.

[4] Gloria Brush, email message to author, March 31, 2014. (A minimal number of editorial changes were made to her message.)

Life-Giving Leaders Drink from Living Water

I received an email from one of my high-level volunteer leaders asking to meet with me as soon as possible. Sensing the urgency of her request, I had my assistant set up an appointment for the following day. My mind raced as I surmised what the emergency could be—a health, marital, or ministry issue? It turned out to be all three.

As she sat across from my desk, an emotional heaviness permeated the air. She began to describe how physically and emotionally exhausted she felt. Between her full-time job, her family, and her volunteer ministry responsibilities, she hadn't had a date night with her husband in months. Not only was she tired and weary, but my friend had a history of depression, and the fatigue and stress were causing depressive symptoms to appear.

And then she dropped the bombshell: she was burned out and needed to step down from her ministry position. We wept and prayed together. I asked God to heal her and provide a season of rest and renewal, trusting him to refresh and restore her.

When she left my office, I was stunned and disappointed, and frankly, I felt like I had failed her. I can't tell you the impact her resignation had on me. This woman had been one of my most capable leaders. She could reproduce leaders and had a great strategic mind. She was life-giving and loved Jesus with all her heart. She had been under my leadership for several years, and we had developed a wonderful friendship. As her friend, I knew it was the best decision for her to step down and rest, but as the ministry leader, I knew the impact her resignation would have on her area of ministry and the added responsibility that would leave on my shoulders.

I sat at my desk for a while and contemplated her decision. She loved the people she served, and she was passionate about the ministry. She was ministering in her sweet spot, her "ten." How did she get to the perpetual state of stress, with her energy depleted and her family relationships and health at risk? Clearly, she was suffering from two major effects of stress: burnout and depression. Stress is inherent in leadership, and how we manage it is one of the determining factors of our productivity and longevity. In this chapter, we're going to look at the effects of stress and how we can pace ourselves so we can run the race the Lord has set before us. Let's dig in.

I did a Google search for the definition of *stress*, and there are . . . drumroll . . . hundreds of *millions* of results. So I used the first result, which defines stress, when used as a noun, as "a state of mental or emotional strain or tension resulting from adverse or very demanding circumstances." As a verb, stress means, "The cause of mental or emotional strain or tension." The Latin word for stress is *strictus*, which means drawn tight.[1]

Having been a licensed mental health therapist for ten years prior to going into full-time ministry, I saw that stress was a common denominator found in many of my clients' mental health issues. In fact, many people are unaware of the effects of negative stressors on their emotional, physical, and spiritual well-being.

The Negative Effects of Stress

Each person in leadership has a certain amount of stress. Stress can't be avoided completely. However, when stress is unmanaged, it can lead to serious health problems. The impact on our health may include high blood pressure, heart disease, obesity, diabetes, headaches, muscle tension or pain, chest pain, fatigue, changes in sex drive, stomach upsets, and sleep problems. Not only does it affect us physically, but when stress goes unchecked, it can affect our mental health, too, causing anxiety, restlessness, lack of motivation or focus, irritability or anger, and sadness or depression. Our behavior can be impacted as well, and we find ourselves overeating or undereating, having angry outbursts, abusing drugs or alcohol, using tobacco, and becoming socially isolated.[2]

Depression is a major mental health issue for women. Catherine Weber, PhD, writes in her article "Women and Depression": "Women are three times as likely as men to be impacted by major depression and dysthymia, starting in adolescence and peaking between the ages of 25 and 45, during the childbearing years."[3] There are many causes of depression, but stress can be a major trigger.

The symptoms of depression range from feeling sad for no particular reason to feeling numb. You feel like your emotional reserves are depleted and your physical energy is low. You may have a lack of interest in things you used to find enjoyable. You feel like isolating yourself from the world. You may overeat or do just the opposite and lose your appetite. You may feel fatigue and just want to curl up in a ball and sleep all day. You may feel anxious, easily irritated, and not able to concentrate.

If this list describes you, there is hope. First, you need to find a qualified, licensed Christian therapist to develop a therapy schedule. Your therapist may refer you to a psychiatrist to evaluate your need for an antidepressant medication. But navigating depression involves more than a weekly therapy session and medication. The best results come from a comprehensive approach, which includes exercise and nutrition, rest, strategies for monitoring stress, and therapeutic and spiritual exercises to help you rediscover meaning and purpose for your life.

I write about depression not only from professional experience; it's very personal for me. I have dysthymia, a mild but long-term form of depression. Dysthymia is chronic and lasts at least two years or longer. About a year after our daughter was born, I found myself feeling sad for no apparent reason. If you were to look at my circumstances, there wasn't any reason for the overwhelming heaviness I was experiencing. We were doing well financially. Our children were happy and healthy. We were involved in a great church with wonderful friends. We were building our first house, but I wasn't able to get myself out of the prevailing dark mood I was experiencing. And my feelings felt familiar. I had battled these feelings since I was a child, but now I had three children to care for, and the feelings of sadness were becoming unmanageable.

I knew I needed professional help. So I went to my doctor, and he prescribed an antidepressant. I'm not a proponent of medication for every physical issue or mental health issue, but for me, the antidepressant was a godsend. I honestly had never felt an overall sense of well-being. It made a huge difference in my life. My husband and children noticed a marked difference in my mood and outlook.

Over the years, therapy, as well as managing my medication, has helped me tremendously. Yes, there have been periods when I've chosen to reduce my antidepressant, but eventually I go to what I call my "dark place." I have a physiological imbalance in my brain, so medication is what I've chosen to help manage my mental health and stay healthy. Honestly, I hesitated whether to write about my struggle with dysthymia, but I want to be part of a movement to remove the stigma associated with mental health issues. So many women deal with depression and struggle in shame or in isolation. On the other hand, many of my clients, women I pastor, as well as friends, manage their depression and have fulfilling lives. And thankfully, the church at large is beginning to openly discuss mental health issues as well as provide counseling services by licensed professionals.

These seven strategies will help you not only manage depression but also maintain a healthy lifestyle.

- Make sure to get adequate sleep and rest.
- Process your feelings through writing, journaling, painting, or music.
- Learn effective ways to manage conflict and difficult emotions.
- Counter negative self-talk with accurate self-talk.
- Develop healthy friendships.
- Be aware of early signs of depression and take steps necessary to stay healthy.[4]

Stress as a Positive Learning Tool

Stress can be a positive, valuable learning tool. In Florida, the construction of the houses is different compared to other regions of the country. Homes in Florida are built to withstand hurricanes. Having built our home, I was amazed by the building process. Cinder blocks provide the external framework, while steel rods are placed in the cinder blocks and cemented to provide a structure that can endure hurricane force winds. What most fascinated me, however, is the way the roofs are constructed. Stacks of clay tiles are strategically placed along the roof and left to sit for several days. The purpose of stacking the tiles is so the foundation and framework acclimate to the weight of the heavy clay tiles. Once this process is complete and enough time has passed for the house to handle the extra weight, the clay tiles are laid accordingly and the roof is completed.

I believe the clay tiles are analogous to stress. Just like the foundation of the house needs to be strengthened in order to withstand the weight of the clay tiles, we need a certain amount of stress to help us gain emotional, physical, and spiritual strength. For example, my daughter takes several advanced placement classes in high school. She is learning that if she doesn't get enough sleep and maintain a reasonable and consistent study routine, she will not adequately meet the homework requirements necessary to pass. The stress of the workload is teaching her the importance of managing her time.

My husband and I often coach church planters, and at one such meeting, the lead pastor of a new church plant was sharing with us the struggles he was experiencing with one of his team members. One of his key leaders decided the emotional and financial stress of church planting was too great and resigned. Understandably, this pastor was devastated. As we consoled him, we shared with him the importance of learning to carry the weight of the church. Just like the foundation of the house had to be strong enough for the weight of the clay tiles, this pastor had to learn to carry the weight of leadership and manage the stress inherent in it. He had to learn to be comfortable with a certain amount of tension. It is our ability to manage stress that determines whether our emotional, physical, and spiritual foundation will withstand life's stressors.

How to Manage Stress: Drink from the Living Water

As a type A personality, I thrive on setting goals and completing projects. I have a list of accomplishments and achievements that, when I look back on it, makes me weary to think about. I love to plan and create, which causes me to think and live in the future rather than in the present moment. There are times when I have to scream at myself to enjoy the moment and focus on what is in front of me.

Performance has always been significantly tied to my self-worth, and I have paid the price both physically and emotionally. A few years ago, I was working as a therapist at an all-girls school, seeing clients in my private practice, writing this book as well as other articles, and volunteering at church. I had just moved my parents into an assisted living facility because dad had terminal cancer, and my two youngest children were in their teens with very active lives. Like so many women in my generation, I was taking care of my parents as well as my children, and to top it all off . . . I was in the beginnings of menopause. My plate was full . . . actually, my platter was full!

Being a people pleaser, I was trying to take care of everyone, not drop any plates, and keep everyone's schedules running smoothly. Yes, I know. You are probably thinking, "Was this woman insane?" Not certifiable but close. Eventually, I realized I was burned out (duh). I just wanted to stop everything, curl up on my couch, watch soap operas, and eat junk. Joy and peace became elusive. While my love for the Lord did not wane, my spiritual life suffered. It diminished to inconsistent times of deep worship and prayer. Most days my prayer time took place in the car on the way to work, to and from appointments, in worship services, and at church events. I knew I had to make changes.

As a therapist, I had helped countless people manage stress, but now I needed help. I went straight to the source, the Bible. I had read the story of Jesus, Mary, and Martha countless times, but I needed to get the essence of this story from my "knower" into my heart. Just as a reminder, let's look at the story in Luke 10:40–41. "But Martha was distracted by the big dinner she was preparing. She came to Jesus and said, 'Lord, doesn't it seem unfair to you that my sister just sits here while I do all the work? Tell her to come and help me.' But the Lord said to her, 'My dear Martha, you are worried and upset over all these details!'"

When reading how Mary sat at the feet of Jesus while Martha busied herself preparing dinner, I had flashbacks to several scenarios from my life, beginning in childhood. One of the messages I internalized growing up in my family was *relaxation equals laziness.* This led to arguments with my younger sister over chores. If she was watching TV instead of cleaning, I would get angry with her. Then when I got married, if my husband, Mark, was lying on the couch and I was in the kitchen cleaning up or preparing a meal, I would resent him and develop an attitude. Sadly, I empathized with Martha . . . I *was* a "Martha." Most women who are performance-driven are Marthas, and I definitely fell into that category. Thankfully, by God's grace, I am much better than I used to be, but I had to be intentional in my quest to learn to "just be." So, how do those of us who are more like Martha become more like Mary?

First, it is necessary to understand the importance of honoring the Sabbath. The following passage from Hebrews shifted my paradigm on the importance of rest.

> For all who have entered into God's rest have rested from their labors, just as God did after creating the world. So let us do our best to enter that rest. But if we disobey God, as the people of Israel did, we will fall. For the word of God is alive and powerful. It is sharper than the sharpest two-edged sword, cutting between soul and spirit, between joint and marrow. It exposes our innermost thoughts and desires. Nothing in all creation is hidden from God. Everything is

> naked and exposed before his eyes, and he is the
> one to whom we are accountable. (Heb. 4:10–13)

Since the Word of God encourages us to *do our best to enter that rest*, let's explore what that looks like. First and foremost, if God had to rest after creating the world, then we need to take a page from his playbook and do the same. I encourage all of my leaders to unplug for one day a week, not only for their own physical, emotional, and spiritual well-being, but also to set an example for those in their spheres of influence. The Sabbath is about spending time with the Lord, focusing on him and letting him refresh you, while you unplug from your work.

One of the reasons I became depressed and burned out a few years ago was that I wasn't consistently taking a day to kick back, rest, and spend time with the Lord. To remedy the situation, I became protective of my day of rest. I found Sundays to be the best day for me to rest. I held my boundary, and if a meeting or event occurred on a Sunday, I respectfully declined the invitation. It felt *so good* to regain control of my schedule and my life. Frankly, it felt good to say no. Remember, saying no to someone does not harm them, but it helps you maintain healthy boundaries. By the way, Sunday does not have to be your day of rest. Currently, my work schedule is Tuesday through Sunday. So Mondays are now my Sabbath, and I love Mondays!

When I read about Mary and Martha, I found something even more intriguing about Mary. The Lord said to Martha in Luke 10:41–42, "My dear Martha, you are worried and upset over all these details! There is only one thing worth being concerned about. Mary has discovered it, and it will not be taken away from her." Mary chose to sit at the feet of Jesus so that she could listen and learn from Jesus. She chose to drink from the living water. I believe Mary had a posture of rest that enabled her to be still, listen, and learn. I personally don't want to miss out on experiencing the promise of his rest mentioned in Hebrews 4:1: "God's promise of entering his rest still stands, so we ought to tremble with fear that some of you might fail to experience it."

Mark and I have three children, two awesome sons and one sweet daughter. All of our children were highly active when they were young. When we needed to instruct or discipline them, we made them stop, look us in the eyes, and repeat our instruction. We did that so our children would learn to listen and receive our instruction. We had to be intentional and faithful to teach them to be still, listen, and learn.

As adults, we need to do the same. We weren't created for constant activity and never-ending noise. We need to practice silence and stillness. But in order to do this, we have to manage our time, create margins in our schedules, and intentionally find balance in our lives. I firmly believe that we cannot run the race that we are called to run if we are overworked and out of balance, with no margins in our lives. When we are exhausted, our emotional defenses are weakened and it's easy to turn to unhealthy habits and temptations. For example, some people turn to comfort foods, becoming overweight and putting their health at risk. How many times do we hear of a church leader having an emotional or physical affair because he or she didn't have time to invest in his or her marriage, became exhausted, and fell into sin? Here are a few ideas that will help you on your journey to a balanced, healthier life.

Take a Sabbath, as already mentioned. Make it nonnegotiable. Unplug from social media and emails so you can plug in to rest. Make sure you spend time with the Lord through prayer, worship, and/or reading the Scriptures.

Schedule margins into your calendar. I know many women with full calendars who schedule exercise, devotional time, and date nights.

Practice the essentials. Drink from the living water through worship, Bible reading, prayer, fasting, and meditating on Scripture.

Practice just being. I know this sounds weird, but you should try to master just being—being okay with inactivity. Our attention is split throughout the day between family, work, and social media. We are inundated with noise and activity. In our stress-filled lives, we need to create time to rest our minds. We need to create headspace. For example, try sitting on a park bench, drinking in the beauty around you. Take a walk, not for the sake of exercise, but just for the sheer joy of being outside, and resist the urge to Instagram your surroundings!

Practice thinking about those things that are worthy of your mental real estate. Philippians 4:8 reminds us, "Fix your thoughts on what is true, and honorable, and right, and pure, and lovely, and admirable. Think about things that are excellent and worthy of praise."

Try deep breathing throughout your workday. Sit in your chair with your feet uncrossed. Relax your shoulders. Shut your eyes so that you're not distracted. When you begin breathing, make yourself aware of your breath going in and out of your mouth and how your lungs fill up and release. If you start thinking about your to-do list, then refocus. When you are deep breathing, shut your eyes and focus on something that brings you joy. I have a special spot in Hilton Head that I think about. It is a bench beside a gorgeous lake. I picture myself sitting on the bench, looking at the water. I remember the way the sun hits the trees around the lake. It is beautiful and I have great memories of family vacations at Hilton Head. The Father gave us imaginations, so how wonderful for us to use our imaginations to calm ourselves, slow our heart rates, breathe . . . and just be.

Listen to soothing music. Music is powerful. It can spur deep emotional reactions in a person. Political and social movements have been driven by music. However, it can also be a great relaxer. In the midst of my workday,

I will often plug my earbuds into my phone and listen to soothing music.

We Can Strengthen Ourselves

We are also able to strengthen ourselves in the Lord even in the darkest and most difficult seasons of our lives. In 1 Samuel 30:1–6, David and his men encountered a horrific sight:

> Then it happened when David and his men came to Ziklag on the third day, that the Amalekites had made a raid on the Negev and on Ziklag, and had overthrown Ziklag and burned it with fire; and they took captive the women and all who were in it, both small and great, without killing anyone, and carried them off and went their way. When David and his men came to the city, behold, it was burned with fire, and their wives and their sons and their daughters had been taken captive. Then David and the people who were with him lifted their voices and wept until there was no strength in them to weep. Now David's two wives had been taken captive, Ahinoam the Jezreelitess and Abigail the widow of Nabal the Carmelite. Moreover David was greatly distressed because the people spoke of stoning him, for all the people were embittered, each one because of his sons and his daughters. But David strengthened himself in the LORD his God. (NASB)

I love the last sentence, "But David strengthened himself in the Lord his God." Just like David, we have the ability to strengthen ourselves in the Lord, even in the midst of pain and heartache, discouragement, exhaustion, or disappointment. We have the capability to set our thoughts on Jesus, strengthening and encouraging ourselves.

We are not created with weak minds. In Acts 24:16, we are encouraged to exercise our consciences. "In view of this, I also do my best to maintain always a blameless conscience both before God and before men" (NASB). We can conclude from this verse that it's our responsibility—not something that just happens to us—to do our best to maintain a blameless conscience. Not only can we exercise our consciences, but we can also take every thought captive. Second Corinthians 10:5 says, "We are destroying speculations and every lofty thing raised up against the knowledge of God, and we are taking every thought captive to the obedience of Christ" (NASB).

As we bring this chapter to a close, it's important to remember that we live in a state of tension between giving our all for the cause of Christ and resting in him. It seems like two opposite actions . . . giving our all and resting in him. I remember reading Jeremiah 2:13, "For my people have done two evil things: They have abandoned me—the fountain of living water. And they have dug for themselves cracked cisterns that can hold no water at all!" We can choose to do life out of our own strength and resources, or we can choose to drink from

Jesus's well of living water, where his yoke is easy and his burden is light.

There is one more warning, one more instance in Scripture where God exhorts his children to enter his rest and not do things on their own or in their own strength. We find these powerful verses in Isaiah 30:15–16: "This is what the Sovereign Lord, the Holy One of Israel, says: 'Only in returning to me and resting in me will you be saved. In quietness and confidence is your strength. But you would have none of it. You said, 'No, we will get our help from Egypt. They will give us swift horses for riding into battle.' But the only swiftness you are going to see is the swiftness of your enemies chasing you!" How often in our culture do we hear "No pain, no gain," and "God helps those who help themselves"? In truth, God accomplished everything for us on the cross. I want to encourage you to sit down and rest in the finished work of Jesus on the cross, so that you can finish the race. Pace yourself, rest in him, so you can complete the call of God on your life.

Small Group Discussion Questions

Life-Giving Leaders Drink from Living Water

1. Have you ever experienced burnout? If so, what were the causes?

2. How has stress been a learning tool in your life?

3. As a leader, when have you felt pressure and stress?

4. How has stress impacted the physical, emotional, and spiritual areas of your life?

5. How do you manage your stress?

6. Do you identify with Mary or Martha?

7. What message did you learn in your childhood about rest and relaxation? Does that message live up to the Word of God?

8. How do you rest? When is your Sabbath?

9. On a scale of 1 to 10, with 10 being the best and 1 being the worst, how would you rate yourself on your ability to be still and listen to your internal world? If your number is low, why is it low? What can you do to make progress in this area of your life?

10. What weaknesses, if any, do you exhibit when you are tired? Do you eat? Yell? Sleep?

11. When was the last time you took a walk just for pleasure?

12. How do you strengthen yourself in the Lord?

Notes

[1] "Stress," *Google*, accessed January 6, 2013, https://www.google.com/#q=definition=of=stress.

[2] Mayo Clinic Staff, "Stress Symptoms: Effects on Your Body and Behavior," *Mayo Clinic*, July 19, 2013, http://www.mayoclinic.org/healthy-living/stress-management/in-depth/stress-symptoms/art-20050987.

[3] Catherine Hart Weber, "Women and Depression," *Christian Counseling Today* 13(2005): 40.

[4] Ibid., 41.

7

Life-Giving Leaders Trust He Is Infinitely More

Trading Your Dreams for His

My earliest memory of praying was as a little girl. Standing outside on our brick patio that my dad had built, I remember looking up into the starry night sky and praying for my future husband. My dream was to have a family of my own, and instinctively I knew to take this dream to God. Several years later, I married Mark, and we had three children who passionately love Jesus. That prayer was the first of thousands of prayers that I have lifted before the Father for my family. Ephesians 3:20 says, "Now all glory to God, who is able, through his mighty power at work within us, to accomplish infinitely more than we might ask or think."

My sisters and I were all theater junkies. We were involved in theater groups at school and in our local community. We loved all the different genres—dramas, musicals, comedies—it didn't matter. If it was on stage, we loved it. For most families, the Super Bowl was the big television event of the year, but for us it was the Tony Awards and the Oscars. I would sit on the couch watching the Oscars with my dad, who was a movie buff, feeling like I was right there in the midst of the show. I would fantasize about winning an Oscar one day and practice my acceptance speech in front of the mirror. My dream was to become an actor and director. I set my sights on a degree in the performing arts, and my goal was to move to New York after college and audition for plays.

God's dream for me was different than mine, and so much better. Between my freshman and sophomore years of college, Jesus captured my heart, and I became his. No longer did I hunger to make it big in the theater; my heart's desire was to serve him in full-time ministry. My once-passionate dream to pursue a life as an actor and director became the passionate pursuit of his dream for me. And it was during this time that I met Mark. We both dreamed of being married and having a family. Mark and I fell in love, married after college, and began our life together as husband and wife. My childhood dream had come true. God answered my prayer, and I was well on my way to having a family.

But . . . that was the only dream Mark and I shared. He grew up in a family where the topic of discussion around the dinner table was business. His mom owned a thriving accounting business as a CPA, and his dad had his own lumber and landscaping business. Naturally, Mark's dream was to be successful in business. Mine was for us to be in full-time ministry. Not knowing how to navigate this marital issue in a healthy way, we argued. I pushed and pushed and manipulated, and I tried every which way to get him to want to go into ministry. I even . . . please don't judge me . . . took him to visit the campus of Asbury Seminary before we were married, to see if he would get "the call" to go into ministry.

Looking back, I can't believe I did that . . . but I did. I own it. I simply couldn't understand how he would want to spend the best hours of his life making money in advertising rather than pastoring a church. It was beyond me. It never occurred to me until years later how selfish I was. Mark was a Christ follower, on his way to being a loving husband and an amazing father, and yet it wasn't enough for me.

When our dreams didn't line up, an undercurrent of disappointment developed in our marriage. I had a decision to make. I could either live in a perpetual state of disappointment, or I could lay down my dream of ministry and embrace my marriage, choose Mark's perspective, honor him, and embrace life as the wife of a man called to the marketplace. I didn't really know how to do this. Laying down this dream felt like I was denying who I was, and it scared me. Like so many times in my life, I knew I needed help.

I called a friend of mine who was several years older than me. Her husband had been in business, became a lay pastor, and then became a full-time paid pastor. She had four children and more life experience than I did. When I met with her, she shared a nugget of priceless wisdom that transformed the way I thought, and it changed the way I approached my marriage and life. She said, "Julia, if you live your life chasing spiritual pursuits but lose your husband and children in the process, then it will have all been in vain." Her words spoke to the depths of my being. I knew it was truth, but more importantly, I knew I had to make major changes in my thinking.

It became evident to me that I was focusing more on the dream of full-time ministry than on following Jesus Christ. Ministry was my idol. I knew I needed to lay down my dream of full-time ministry. At that time, I didn't know that his dream for us was infinitely greater than anything I could think or imagine. I just knew I was laying down a dream that was seemingly embedded into the very fiber of who I was. So I prayed, and prayed, and prayed some more. I declared to the Lord that I was going to be the best wife and mother I knew how to be by supporting Mark's thriving career in advertising and raising our three children.

At that point, an incredible transformation occurred in my heart. I experienced a peace that surpassed understanding. When I gave up my dream, my agenda, and my plans, our marriage became more loving and less contentious. Mark felt less pressured to be and do something he didn't feel called to. Over the next several years, Mark experienced remarkable success in newspaper advertising, and I was right by his side, praying for him and fully supporting his dream. We enjoyed all the perks of success, a beautiful home, great vacations, private schools, medical and dental care. I went to graduate school and became a mental health therapist.

But then everything changed. The economic downturn occurred, and the newspaper industry took a major hit. Many newspapers closed their doors or downsized. Like many senior executives, Mark found himself out of a job. The next several years were spent trying to financially survive. We tried to purchase a business, which didn't work out. Mark did consulting, sold insurance, and even worked for a repo company. But out of this challenging season in our lives, God birthed a new dream in Mark's heart.

Mark began to crave a new direction and purpose for his life. He spent hours reading the Bible and praying. He felt a deep longing in his heart to serve on staff at our local church, helping our lead pastor execute the vision God had given him. Now Mark works on staff as a pastor at Bayside Community Church. If Mark had gone into ministry when I wanted him to, it would have been because I pressured him.

Amazing, isn't it? God fulfilled my dream infinitely more than I could think or imagine, in his time and in his way. Once I realized that ministry was an idol, I laid down that dream. I was content to support Mark's desire to be in business. My goal was to live my life as a healthy Christ follower, with a loving marriage and happy, thriving children.

I learned so many lessons from that season in our lives. First, holding a dream so tightly that it robs you of relationships and hinders your ability to trust the Lord with your life is not a dream worth having. Second, ministry is not the goal—Jesus is. Third, laying your dream down gives God the opportunity to fulfill his dream for your life, in his time. Finally, I learned that God will always do infinitely more than I can imagine.

In this situation, God was so good to bless me with my dream of having a family but also my dream of Mark being in full-time ministry. But what happens when your dream isn't his dream?

When Your Dream Isn't His Dream

After becoming a Christ follower, I started attending a church that focused on church planting. The lead pastor and his wife were part of teams that planted churches in the United States, Africa, and Europe. Their lives were full of relationships, excitement, and adventure, and most importantly, people's lives were changed through the church plants. Years later, Mark and I began attending a thriving local church plant, Bayside Community Church. We fell in love with Bayside. Its life-giving atmosphere is the reason it's one of the healthiest churches in America today.

Church planters are my heroes. It takes a tremendous amount of courage and tenacity to leave family and friends, move to a new community, and plant a church. The idea itself sounds thrilling, but the realities of planting are arduous and difficult. The stress it puts on couples, both because of the financial risk and the time it takes to invest in people and build leaders and teams, is not for the faint of heart. However, the eternal rewards far outweigh the pain of planting—eternal destinations are changed from hell to heaven, families are restored, marriages are strengthened, relationships are developed, and communities are blessed.

This became my dream. Everything about church planting resonated in my soul. It was the engine of my life. The vision for church planting was the topic of my conversations. When we'd drive to a new town, I would think, "Is there a life-giving church here? Would this be a good community to plant a church?" It became my passion. If someone asked me what was on my bucket list, it wasn't traveling the world or building a dream house, it was planting a church.

Little did I know that Mark was also thinking and praying about planting a church. When he told me, I was ecstatic. I thought . . . this is it . . . we're really going to do this! We both had the same vision. We even had the city picked out. I kept thinking how wonderful it was that we were going to be planting and building together. I was beyond excited. We truly believed it was a God-dream.

Over the next several months, we had long talks about church planting. We prayed and asked God to make it clear if this was his dream for our lives. We firmly believe that God speaks through spiritual authority, which in our case is our pastor. Subsequently, our next step in the process was to seek wise counsel from our pastors. We came to the conclusion that our lead pastor's vision for the local church was larger than ours. We settled in our hearts that we were called to Bayside and the vision of our lead pastor. We determined that we actually had greater influence in the local church where we were planted and could live out the call of God on our lives than if we ventured into a church plant.

We determined that while our dream was a beautiful and wonderful dream, church planting wasn't God's dream for our lives. His dream for us was infinitely better than ours. We were reminded again of the truth of God's Word, Ephesians 3:20, "Now all glory to God, who is able, through his mighty power at work within us, to accomplish infinitely more than we might ask or think." We chose to trade our dream for his, and once again, we experienced peace and freedom to focus on the present. Life-giving leaders trust that he will accomplish in us and through us infinitely more than we might ask or think.

How Do You Know What God's Dream Is for You?

One of the greatest joys of leadership is helping those we lead to find their God-given passion. A key mark of a life-giving leader is that he or she freely gives ministry away. In other words, if I have ministry or leadership opportunities that I know would benefit someone in the sphere of influence God has given me, then I give that opportunity to them. For example, several of the women's leaders who report to me dream of helping women trapped in human trafficking. We have several ministries in our community that help combat this horrible injustice. So I've connected these ladies with those ministry opportunities. But what happens when someone doesn't know her God-given dream? How can we as life-giving leaders help people discover their dreams?

I'm often asked the following questions, "How do I know what God wants me to do with my life?" "How do I know what my purpose is?" "People talk about having a purpose and destiny, but how do I know what mine is?" These are wonderful questions to wrestle with and worthy of your time to determine the answers.

The i3 Lab

As I mentioned in Chapter Two, I wanted to help people find their passion and purpose, so I developed the i3 Lab. The three I's are: *inspire*, *innovate*, and *initiate*. The i3 Lab is divided into three parts. Part one is designed to *inspire* you to help you discover your "sweet spot," your "10," what God has uniquely gifted you for. Part two is designed to help you develop *innovative* ways to carry out your calling and use your passions in the local church. Part three is designed to help you take *initiative* and implement your dream in the local church. I want to do a mini i3 Lab with you to help you move closer to God's purpose for your life. Before we begin, I want to lay a foundation by exploring the parable of the talents in Matthew 25:14–30:

Again, the Kingdom of Heaven can be illustrated by the story of a man going on a long trip. He called together his servants and entrusted his money to them while he was gone. He gave five bags of silver to one, two bags of silver to another, and one bag of silver to the last—dividing it in proportion to their abilities. He then left on his trip.

The servant who received the five bags of silver began to invest the money and earned five more. The servant with two bags of silver also went to work and earned two more. But the servant who received the one bag of silver dug a hole in the ground and hid the master's money.

After a long time their master returned from his trip and called them to give an account of how they had used his money. The servant to whom he had entrusted the five bags of silver came forward with five more and said, "Master, you gave me five bags of silver to invest, and I have earned five more."

The master was full of praise. "Well done, my good and faithful servant. You have been faithful in handling this small amount, so now I will give you many more responsibilities. Let's celebrate together!"

The servant who had received the two bags of silver came forward and said, "Master, you gave me two bags of silver to invest, and I have earned two more."

The master said, "Well done, my good and faithful servant. You have been faithful in handling this small amount, so now I will give you many more responsibilities. Let's celebrate together!"

Then the servant with the one bag of silver came and said, "Master, I knew you were a harsh man, harvesting crops you didn't plant and gathering crops you didn't cultivate. I was afraid I would lose your money, so I hid it in the earth. Look, here is your money back."

But the master replied, "You wicked and lazy servant! If you knew I harvested crops I didn't plant and gathered crops I didn't cultivate, why didn't you deposit my money in the bank? At least I could have gotten some interest on it."

Then he ordered, "Take the money from this servant, and give it to the one with the ten bags of silver. To those who use well what they are given, even more will be given, and they will have an abundance. But from those who do nothing, even what little they have will be taken away. Now throw this useless servant into outer darkness, where there will be weeping and gnashing of teeth."

Notice the servant who buried his talent was thrown into outer darkness. I've often wondered why he chose to bury his talent. This is what I've determined. He buried his talent because it was safer than taking a risk. It's also easier to bury a talent than to work toward increase. Therefore, I believe this servant chose not to use his talent because he was fearful and lazy. Before doing this mini lab, you will need to determine not to let fear keep you safe and inhibit you from using your gifts and talents.

Think of fear as a cage. The cage will keep you boxed safely in your comfort zone, but it will also inhibit you from living dangerously for Christ and from living a fulfilled life. Ephesians 2:10 says, "For we are God's masterpiece. He has created us anew in Christ Jesus, so we can do the good things he planned for us long ago." Our goal is to do those things he planned for us long ago.

Let's begin. First, I suggest starting a new journal so you can record this process, answer questions, and track the Holy Spirit's work in your life during this mini lab. Scripture says in Habakkuk 2:2, "Then the LORD said to me, 'Write my answer plainly on tablets, so that a runner can carry the correct message to others.'"

Part One: Inspire

Mission Statement

The first step in pursuing your passion is to define that passion. You do this by adding a framework in the form of a mission statement. As you develop your mission statement, I want you to focus on what you wish to be and do based on the values and principles that undergird your beliefs and actions. God has a wonderful plan for your life. He wants you to serve him using the gifts and talents he has placed within you.

Before we begin working on your mission statement, I have several exercises that I want you to do to get your creative juices flowing and help you listen to your internal world.

Exercise One: The Candle

Imagine a lit candle. The wick in the candle has only a few more hours to burn. The wick in the candle represents the amount of time you have left to live on this earth. The candle is burning, which means the wick is getting shorter. Something else you should know about the candle: it is scented. It emits an aroma which permeates the atmosphere. Now ask yourself the following questions.

1. What do I want to do with the life I have left to live?
2. How do I want to live my life?
3. What do I want to experience, witness, and learn?
4. What do I want to change?
5. What do I want to do in ministry?
6. What segment of the population am I drawn to? Children? Adolescents? Adults? All ages?
7. What kind of aroma do I want to leave? A beautiful scent that reminds my loved ones of beautiful memories? A powerful scent that reminds people to press on and lean in? Describe your own.

Exercise Two: The News

When doing this exercise, focus and reflect on your life and legacy. Now imagine you are reading a newspaper or your favorite online news outlet. You are sitting at your desk at the office or in your special chair in your family room, and you read a headline which says you have passed away. Write the article following the headline. Include in the article how you want to be remembered, relationships that were important to you, and your accomplishments.

Exercise Three: Garbage Pile

In our community, we have two garbage landfills. You'll regret it if you drive anywhere near them with the windows down! Now imagine you are in the bottom of a pile of garbage with one hand sticking out, and you are yelling for help. What bags of garbage do you need removed in order for you to fulfill your dream, determine your passion, and live a fulfilling life? Is it unforgiveness, bitterness, or procrastination? What weighs you down?

Exercise Four: Obstacle Course

Imagine yourself competing in a race filled with obstacles; perhaps there is a pit of quicksand, an eight-foot wall to climb and jump over, and a pool of water filled with piranhas. Each obstacle represents a challenge in your life that keeps you from comprehending all that God has for you. Maybe the obstacle is your debt load, and you need to remove this obstacle to move closer to your dream.

Think about the obstacles that need to be removed, and write them down. Then write down the steps you will take to remove these obstacles.

Exercise Five: The Banquet Table

Picture yourself at your favorite restaurant. On one side of the table is a group of waiters bringing you your favorite meal, attending to your needs, and providing you with excellent service. On the other side of the table is a group of waiters doing the exact opposite. This group is taking the food away from your table, ignoring your needs, and providing horrible service.

The waiters represent the following: those people who add to or take away from your life, those tasks that add to or take away from your life, and those activities that add to or take away from your life. For example, one of my time-suckers is watching television, while an activity that adds to my life is exercise. Write these down and then pray and determine what and who you need to take out of your life and who or what you need to add to your life.

Your Mission Statement

Now that you've completed exercises one through five, hopefully you are more in tune with your passion and what you value, and you've identified any obstacles standing in the way of pursuing your passion. The next step is to do an exercise that will help you develop your mission statement.

Draw two boxes. Label the first box *Fulfillment* and *Enjoyment*. Label the second box *Frustration* and *Hate*. Please note that there are no right or wrong answers for this exercise. The answers vary from person to person.

In the fulfillment and enjoyment box, write everything you find deeply satisfying and that brings you happiness. For example, you may find fulfillment in teaching people about life-changing spiritual principles or helping others fulfill their potential in Christ. You may like to write, draw, exercise, shop, redo furniture, or feed the homeless.

In the frustration and hate box, list those things that you hate and those things that drain the energy out of you, causing frustration. For example, long projects, things that don't move at a fast pace, clutter, or technology.

Once you're settled with your lists in each box, you can begin to develop your mission statement. When developing your mission statement, utilize those things in your fulfillment and enjoyment box and stay away from those things in your frustration and hate box. A mission statement needs to be focused and simple. I encourage you to make it short and to the point so you can remember it. Make it general enough so it applies to the many seasons of your life. The primary benefit of your mission statement is that it will help you say yes to those opportunities that line up with your mission statement and no to those that do not. For example, here is my mission statement: "To encourage, direct, and inspire people to reach their full potential." It's simple, to the point, and easy to remember. Amazingly, I get to fulfill this mission statement in various areas of my life: as mother, pastor, therapist, writer, and director of small groups.

Part Two: Innovate

Part Two is designed to help you marry your passion with the practical side of life. The instructions for this part are to dream big, don't think about the "how," and go where you've never gone before! Have fun and explore and create innovative ideas. I want to encourage you to stay away from playing the devil's advocate with your ideas. In other words, this is not the time to consider the "what if this happens or doesn't happen" type of thoughts. Just dream. Let the creative juices flow!

To help you get started, here are a few of the innovative ideas I came up with when I did this exercise: public speaking, writing books, full-time ministry, and helping people find their right fit (or "10") in the local church and in their professions. As a side note to encourage you, all of these dreams have come true. My mission statement helped me focus on the main thing, and my list of innovative ideas helped me think of new possibilities and dream big.

Part Three: Initiate

Now it's time to think through the nuts and bolts of how to make your dreams happen. Before we move forward, remember to surrender your dreams to him, asking him to direct your steps. Proverbs 16:9 says, "We can make our plans, but the LORD determines our steps."

First, write your dreams in one column. In the next column, write steps toward making your dreams happen. I want to share my list with you. I did these exercises in 2008, and at the time I was working as a mental health therapist. I was volunteering at my local church leading women's small groups and speaking occasionally at women's events. I was not writing.

Dreams	Steps
Write book	Attend writers' conference, write a book proposal
Full-time ministry	Faithfully serve in small groups, disciple others
Public speaking	Seek opportunities, learn effective communication techniques

Once you have completed this final exercise, it's a great idea to put deadlines next to your steps. For example, if your dream is to run a half marathon, then your steps would involve developing a running routine, registering for a marathon, and then training for the marathon.

For each dream you accomplish, make sure to celebrate. Life is full of trials and challenges; we need to remember to celebrate the "infinitely more than we can think or imagine" that God gives us. When I had my first article published, my family took me out to dinner. I want to encourage you to celebrate and give thanks to the Author of your dreams.

Small Group Discussion Questions

Life-Giving Leaders Trust He Is Infinitely More

1. Do you remember the first time you prayed? If so, share about that experience.

2. What was your first dream?

3. Share when you have experienced Ephesians 3:20 in your life.

4. Share about a time in your life when God's dream was different than your dream.

5. Share your journey doing the i3 Lab. What exercise was most challenging? What exercise was most helpful?

6. Share your mission statement.

7. What steps are you going to take to help you move toward your dreams?

8. How will you celebrate the fruition of each dream?

9. When have you helped someone else experience his or her dream?

Navigating the Male-Dominated Church World

The hard truths presented in this chapter may touch off a few nerves. That's okay. We need our collective feathers ruffled. From head coverings to whether a woman should preach from the pulpit, the topic of women in church leadership has long been a source of contention within Christendom. The objective of this chapter is not to do a theological study on the role of women in church leadership but rather to glean valuable lessons from women leaders and their vastly different experiences. Out of respect for the women whose stories I share, I have changed their names with the exception of Jenni Catron, who graciously provided an interview for this chapter.[1]

I also want to provide an honest, authentic, realistic, and perhaps not wholly politically correct male perspective on this topic. Pastor Mark Mateer, my husband and pastor at Bayside Community Church, and Pastor Sean Callaghan, my friend and Director of Discipleship at Bayside Community Church, will share their unique perspectives from working with female colleagues in ministry.

Betrayal: Karyn

When the church grew to twelve hundred members, Karyn began her tenure as the first paid Women's Ministry Director where her husband served as associate pastor. Thinking the church was progressive by embracing women in leadership positions, she soon found out that an invisible dynamic existed in the church's DNA. This invisible dynamic said, "We appreciate you, but stay in your place." The core stance of the church was that women were excluded from areas of leadership other than women's ministry. This particular church culture negated a woman's voice. This was particularly surprising because Karyn and the senior pastor had discussed the topic of women in church leadership, and he supported women preaching from the pulpit.

The senior pastor initiated a yearlong discussion with church elders about women in leadership, with the expectation of arriving at an answer by the end of the year. He invited Karyn to be a part of the discussion. However, Karyn found the meetings awkward and tense, with an adversarial atmosphere permeating the meetings. Some people threatened to stop tithing if women were instituted in leadership positions.

During this time, an influential elder and his wife brought a complaint to the senior pastor about Karyn. A campaign to oust her ensued, led by this woman and her cohorts, who never spoke with Karyn about their concerns. When the women didn't get their desired outcome, their husbands got involved. At that point, both Karyn and her husband offered to resign. Refusing to accept their resignation, the senior pastor restructured the church organization, making her husband an executive pastor. This move infuriated the adversarial group. Feeling pressured, the senior pastor asked Karyn to step down from her position. Devastated and feeling betrayed, both Karyn and her husband resigned.

This experience was excruciatingly painful for Karyn and her husband. Leaving their positions meant leaving their church. They lost friends and suffered financially. She and her husband had to rebuild their lives. Forgiveness was difficult. She realized there was no formula for forgiveness, just a lot of raw conversations with God, spewing out all the venom toward the people involved. She grieved all that was lost and lamented to God from the depth of her pain. After a long healing process, Karyn is now actually grateful for the trajectory of her life. The following is a list of valuable lessons she learned about herself and about leadership.

- It is important to do the hard work of self-evaluation, and take responsibility for her contributions to the scenario. She realized that she tended to flatter others and be a people pleaser. The situation caused her to look at her own self-deception.

- It is important to keep short records, and quickly deal with relational issues. Don't bury stuff with people.
- Karyn learned to advocate for herself and realized there was a point where she had to say, "I'm not going to take this anymore." She wanted to engage the women involved but only when her heart was ready. And when she was ready, she called the women, and sadly, none would meet with her. She handwrote notes to them, and finally had meetings, but they did not go well. There was no one there to mediate.
- Lead out of relationship. Leaders need committed relationships with the people they serve.
- Senior pastors need to honor relationships. When anxiety and pressure come, you can't throw people under the bus. Absolutely lead with integrity and honesty. Don't tell people what they want to hear, but what is honest.

Stereotyping: Sharon

Now, let's look at Sharon's experience. Sharon is the children's pastor at her church. She is fully supported by her senior pastor; however, as you will read, she was stereotyped by a group of men outside her church setting.

Sharon arrived at the board meeting without pen and paper, not in disregard for the importance of recording the happenings, but rather to keep from sending the wrong signal. She was asked to be a board member by her senior pastor, who had neither the time nor the patience to do so. Her church was looking to make significant changes in this struggling nonprofit organization because they saw promise.

She sat at the table with ten men; she had spent the past year getting to know them and earning their respect. They had arrived to nominate and elect officers. She arrived with her church's desire that she run for vice chairman or chairman. First up was the appointing of a secretary and treasurer.

The long pause after the announcement for nominations gave her concern. As she glanced up from the table, she noticed that all ten men were looking in her direction. She tried to hide the anger that began boiling up inside. She could tell by their faces what they were thinking. She didn't get to reflect too long, as the chairman said, "Sharon, as the only lady here, I think you'd be great as the secretary and treasurer." She couldn't believe he had said it out loud and within her presence. The other guys quickly jumped in and elected her. Her fate was sealed. It was a long year for Sharon of serving in this undesirable position, knowing she was there because she was a woman. She did attend each meeting, and she did the job she had been assigned with great effort, knowing that she was working as unto the Lord (Col. 3:23–24).

I can relate to Sharon's story. I, too, have attended meetings where events were planned and food needed to be prepared. I averted my eyes from the men in the room, trying not to be assigned this task. It's not that I don't think women—or men, for that matter—should or shouldn't provide food for church events. It's just that I am not a cook. I'd rather purchase food or have an event catered. However, I have several friends who love to cook and are thrilled to use their gifts and talents to provide food for events. I simply don't, and I don't want anyone to *assume* that I should be the one to provide food because I am a woman. Frankly, I'd rather run the event. I love Sharon's heart to serve on the committee as unto the Lord; it's a valuable lesson for anyone to learn and implement.

Encouragement: Jenni

Jenni Catron, co-author of *Just Lead, Clout*, and *The 4 Dimensions of Extraordinary Leadership*, is a rarity in the church world. For several years, she served in executive leadership at Cross Point Church in Nashville before moving to California to take the position of Shared Resources Leader at Menlo Park Presbyterian Church.

Eleven years ago, while working in the music industry, Jenni was a volunteer member of the launch team for Cross Point when Pete Wilson, the lead pastor, asked her to come on staff.

Coming from a corporate environment where there were no established boundaries, Jenni was naïve to church culture. She learned to navigate and create new boundaries as a woman overseeing men as well as the following valuable lessons in her role as an executive leader.

- Pete's perspective toward women on staff focused more on a person's gifts rather than position or gender. His support of Jenni's gifts was critical to her success, particularly since some people left because of her position.
- Jenni and her colleagues had a high level of integrity, trust, and honor for one another. But they used wisdom and accountability in the boundaries between men and women on staff. However, the boundaries were not so strict as to prohibit working with one another.
- Jenni differentiated between organizational meetings and discipleship meetings. Let me explain. There were times when she and Pete needed to have closed-door meetings because the topics were sensitive in nature (i.e., staffing or organizational issues). These were considered work or organizational meetings. However, discipleship meetings were gender-based and had to maintain strict boundaries.
- One way Jenni protected her marriage was by allowing her husband to have access to her schedule and vice versa.

Pete's focus on gifts rather than gender afforded Jenni the opportunity to experience the beauty of brothers and sisters in Christ building and advancing the local church. Unfortunately, not every woman experiences the healthy relational atmosphere and opportunities that Jenni experienced at Cross Point. However, there are men in ministry who view women in leadership as vitally important to the health of the local church. Two of these men are my husband, Pastor Mark Mateer, and Pastor Sean Callaghan, Director of Discipleship at Bayside Community Church. Here are their perspectives on women in church leadership.

Pastor Mark

Mark's background includes twenty-three years in newspaper advertising, which is dominated by a female workforce. Most of his colleagues, supervisors, and employees were women. Throughout his advertising career, he managed several female employees, and had several female managers. Now in full-time paid ministry, several of his staff and volunteers are women. Here are the questions I asked and here are his honest—not always politically correct, but authentic—answers.

How can women in leadership navigate successfully in male-dominated church settings?

Men value people who can help them be successful—it doesn't matter if you are a man or a woman. Men respect good leadership no matter the sex of the leader. If you create an environment where men can do their best work, they don't care if you are a man or woman. If you create an environment where they can't do their best work, then they may blame the fact that you are a woman.

We ask ourselves, "Does this person help me become successful?" The way for a woman to be successful is to understand what her supervisor's goals and aspirations are and help him accomplish those by observing how he spends his time and what he talks about, as well as his concerns. Know his expectations of you. With men, they are not great at expressing what they need, so you have to find out by doing the research.

What are the differences you've experienced between female and male employees or supervisors?

Men have a work world and home world. When they come to the office, they are in their work world, and when they come home, they are in their home world, and they have a social world, too. For most men, we can segment things. So a man can be in the midst of a divorce and still focus on his job because it is easier for him to separate it out. For a woman, it's one world.

When I was managing women, and I experienced poor work performance, I would drill down and find out that something wasn't right at home. If you get the home fixed, then work will fall into place. I, personally, have never experienced this with men. If there is an issue at work, it usually has to do with work. Men are not as complicated. Men seem to get over things and move on more quickly and are not as concerned about social and interpersonal issues.

What other advice can you give that would be valuable to a woman?

You have to understand the work culture that God has placed you in. For example, I work at a church that values hearing God and using wisdom to make decisions. In a corporate setting, it is about making a decision—right or wrong—to move the ball down the field. For a woman to be successful, she needs to understand her work/church environment. Understanding the culture helps her to be successful.

Also, men want women to be feminine. It is not a negative to be feminine in a work environment. Women put it on themselves that they have to be like men to succeed. Men don't think that way; however, men don't like high-maintenance women. By high maintenance, I mean extending meetings by talking too much. Most men value information that is succinct and to the point. Don't overwhelm us with detail. Successful women clearly articulate and define vision and strategy. Men are task-oriented. Updates are good and helpful, but don't overwhelm us with details. Succinct updates are sufficient.

Also, men know they can't discriminate and ask these questions during the interview process about how a woman is going to handle motherhood and her job, but we do *think* about how a woman who has a baby or is pregnant—how this will impact her ability to do her job. It is a legitimate concern, and men are genuinely curious about how women will balance both. So, it's good to articulate a plan during the interview process about child care if your child is sick or maternity leave plans. If there is an issue, acknowledge it and explain how you will work around it. Not acknowledging it does not lead men to think there is not an issue. We still wonder how you will do it; think about and articulate your contingency plans.

Pastor Sean

What is your perspective on women in ministry?

I pray and ask God to help me see a person the way he sees a person. Gender is a factor but not the main factor. Gender is part of that but not the only thing. I believe in an individual's strengths, calling, purpose, and vision, which supersede gender. So in those things I ask the same questions whether male or female. Just because someone is a woman doesn't discount what I think God can do first in her and then through her.

Generally speaking, women are more intuitive, and it seems it is easier for women to hear the Holy Spirit. What are your thoughts on this and how do you handle situations where women leaders approach you with something they believe they have heard from the Lord?

On a broad basis, this is correct; women are more intuitive. Generally, women are more open to hear the Holy Spirit then men. However, on an individual basis, if a woman comes to me and makes the statement that the Holy Spirit showed her something, I will go and pray about that because the same God who spoke to her will speak to me as well. I would treat it the same as if a guy came to me; however, it happens more with women than with men. I take it to God and hear God's voice for myself.

What do you think of women as pastors?

I believe that women can and should be in leadership. Women make up 51 percent of the population and women need to be in leadership. On an individual basis, I see no reason for a woman not to lead a man as long as you have specific guardrails in place to keep healthy boundaries, but you would also have the same guardrails in place if you had a man leading a woman. Generally, men minister to men, women minister to women. However, that's not always practical.

Specifically, I see nothing in the Bible that tells me a woman can't be a pastor, but I don't see a ton of examples of women being pastors, either. It's a shoulder shrug thing. I have very few opinions that aren't biblically based that I would stake my life on because I am always learning and growing. If the Bible isn't clear about something, then I'm going to pray about it, but if the Bible is clear, then that is just the way it is. But I see nothing in the Bible that a woman can't be a pastor, especially if I see the gifting, anointing, and fruit from a pastor such as the equipping of the saints to do the work of the ministry, believing in people, calling forth purpose in a person's life. If it walks like a duck and talks like a duck then that person is a pastor, and if it happens to be a woman, then it's a pastor that is a woman. At the very least, they are pastoring people. The office of pastor won't come to every woman who does these things, but I can't see that the office can't come to a woman who does those things.

How can a woman be more respected and well-received in a church environment? Say a woman wants to get into leadership in a church setting, how does she make this happen?

It is not gender first for me. Number one, a person who wants to be in leadership needs to have a good prayer life. God needs to be number one.

If a person wants to be in leadership in a church that doesn't want her, then I would question, is that really God's will for her? First off, finding an environment that embraces equipping people, both men and women, for the work of the ministry is probably the environment that a woman wants to look for. At some point, she will be fighting an uphill battle if that doesn't exist. I would hate to see a woman waste the opportunity to make a difference in a person's life for eternity by fighting a battle against church authority that has a different point of view. If a woman chooses to put herself in an environment where she is not able to do what God has asked her to do, then choosing that environment may not be good stewardship of what God has called her to do.

What happens if a woman's husband is asking her to stay in a church that doesn't accept women in leadership?

Well, the dynamic of the marriage comes before the dynamic of ministry, and the dynamic of your relationship with God comes before the dynamic of the marriage. If you are in a church environment where your gifts are not accepted, that can be frustrating, but reaching an understanding in your marriage comes first. Often marriages are torn apart because men and women put their ministries before marriage.

What happens when a woman's vision does not match the lead pastor's vision?

The "I'm gonna do what I'm gonna do and you better bless it!" attitude is not honoring. This is an issue for people in general and is not gender-based. You have to honor authority and the vision of the lead pastor. If anyone, man or woman, brings a vision that isn't in harmony with the lead pastor's vision, that causes division and has to be addressed by church leadership. Often these issues have nothing to do with gender but everything to do with heart, character, and attitude. However, when these situations are addressed with men, it tends to be a little quieter, while these situations with women tend to be aired out more publically, trying to get people to side with her. Women are such huge connectors and this can cause a domino effect.

What do you think women have to contend with in a church environment that men don't?

Sexism and bias. There are very few men who have been taught to view women the way they were created to be viewed, with respect and honor, the way that God teaches us we should. Men are taught from a very early age to view women the way they have been trained by their culture unless they have been trained to look at women from a biblical perspective.

Men need men to teach them how to view women, and with so many men being raised without fathers, it's not getting easier for a woman to walk into a scenario and be judged on her merits rather than the way she looks, and whether or not she is flirtatious. Frankly, it goes both ways. If women are not trained to look at men and themselves the way they should, then they enter into a situation doing things they are doing driven by culture in a church setting that shouldn't be. It's an uphill battle for both genders, but definitely more of an uphill battle for a woman than a man in the church world.

How Do Women View Themselves?

Sean's last statement about women viewing themselves via culture triggered me to ask the following question: *How does a woman who walks through the doors of a church for the first time view herself if she is in fact a product of our culture?* The most influential driving force of American culture today is the entertainment industry, with iTunes being a major player in delivering music and its messages to the population at large. Unprecedented access to music on mobile devices keeps the masses plugged into earbuds 24/7. So it's not a stretch to conclude that what people listen to will influence how they view life and themselves.

I researched a few top songs of 2013: Pitbull's "Timber," Lady Gaga's "Do What You Want," and Justin Timberlake's "Suit and Tie." Here is a glimpse at the lyrics.

Timber
Pitbull, featuring Kesha

The bigger they are, the harder they fall
These big-iddy boys are dig-gidy dogs
I have 'em like Miley Cyrus, clothes off
Twerking in their bras and thongs, timber
Face down, booty up, timber
That's the way we like to—what? —timber
I'm slicker than an oil spill
She say she won't but I bet she will, timber

Do What You Want
*Lady Gaga

Do what I want
Do what I want with your body
Do what I want
Do what I want with your body
Back of the club, taking shots, getting naughty
No invitations, it's a private party

*Lady Gaga is viewed as a role model by many women.

Suit and Tie
Justin Timberlake

Stop, let me get a good look at it
So thick, now I know why they call it a fatty
Sh*t so sick got a hit and picked up a habit
That's alright, 'cause you're all mine
Go on and show 'em who you call daddy
I guess they're just mad 'cause girl, they wish they
    had it
My killer, my thriller, yeah you're a classic
And you're all mine tonight

As you can see from reading these lyrics, women are portrayed as sexual objects and often see themselves as sexual objects instead of as women afforded all the honor, dignity, and esteem of a daughter of the King. Here is an idea you won't find in the lyrics of pop culture: in 1 Timothy 5:2, we read, "Treat older women as you would your mother, and treat younger women with all purity as you would your own sisters."

The woman coming through the doors of a life-giving church for the first time needs her mind transformed by the living Word of God, his love, and his grace. She needs to know that Jesus was *the advocate* for women, affording them honor, dignity, and significance. She needs to know that God's Holy Spirit is for men and women, as the Bible says in Joel 2:28–29: "Then, after doing all those things, I will pour out my Spirit upon all people. Your sons and daughters will prophesy. Your old men will dream dreams, and your young men will see visions. In those days I will pour out my Spirit even on servants—men and women alike." She needs the opportunity to serve and worship in life-giving churches where she can be fully equipped to do the works of the ministry in all the fullness that God has for her. This is *life-giving leadership!*

Small Group Discussion Questions

Navigating the Male-Dominated Church World

1. Are your experiences in leadership more like Karyn's, Sharon's, or Jenni's?

2. What personal boundaries do you have when working with male colleagues? Does your church have protocols in place for male/female relationships?

3. What are your thoughts on Pastor Mark's and Pastor Sean's responses to the questions posed in this chapter?

4. If you are married, how has ministry impacted your marriage?

5. Does your church authority support your calling? If not, what are your options?

6. Does your vision for women in ministry fit into your lead pastor's vision?

7. Who or what helped you to form how you view yourself?

8. How can we help our daughters as well as the women we lead to value themselves?

Note

[1]Jenni Catron, email interview used by permission, April 11, 2012.

9
·········

Life-Giving Relationships between Women

The Joys of Leading

There is a scene in the compelling movie *The Help* when Skeeter, a journalist writing about the plight of black maids in the South, walks into one of their homes and finds a group of maids ready to tell their stories of injustice because of the color of their skin. Once hesitant to openly share their stories of cruel discrimination, the group of women, led by maid and Christ follower Aibileen, realized that together their collective voice was more powerful than their individual voices. Their collective story gave power to the Civil Rights Movement. Now, think for a moment how much we as Christian women could collectively accomplish if we caught the vision of the power of unity like the black maids in *The Help*. What could the collective voice of the women in your Christian community accomplish?

For us to move forward in unity, barriers and walls between women must be eradicated. Sadly, many women see other women as threats. We are socialized to dislike one another. We victimize each other as a result of our own emotional hurts. We victimize each other over men. I have seen adolescent girls give up childhood friends over boys, and women commit adultery with their friends' husbands.

As women leaders, transformed by the power of the Holy Spirit, leading in local churches, how can we create healthy relationships where we empower one another instead of competing, uplift one another instead of degrading, and champion each other's accomplishments and callings rather than comparing? How can we model this for the women we lead? These questions require multiple answers, and this chapter will seek to answer these profound and all-important questions so that we as women who love Jesus can unite to impact not only our generation but generations to follow with the gospel of Jesus Christ.

For us to begin to answer this question, we need to gain a better understanding of how women develop, particularly our social development. It's fascinating to see how we develop relationships from infancy through adulthood. Here is a brief overview.

From the moment we take our first gasp of air to the moment we take our last, we go through various developmental stages. Each stage consists of six domains: emotional, physical, social, sexual, intellectual, and spiritual. To better understand the relationships between women, we're going to focus on the social domain. All of the information on the social development of girls comes from my favorite expert on girlhood, JoAnn Deak, PhD. Dr. Deak contends, and I agree with her, that girlhood is divided into nine stages of development. An understanding of how we develop socially as young girls will help us gain a better understanding of how we relate with one another as adult women. The following is her chart on social development.

Stages	Ages
Self-Awareness	Birth–2
Parallel Play	2–3
Interactive Play	3–6
Transitory Friendships	6–8
Friendship Clusters	8–10
Best Friends	10–12
Cliques	12–14
Interest-Based Friendship Groups	14 and older
(Almost) Universal Acceptance	High School Seniors[1]

Next time you're in the church lobby, look at the crowd of women. Observe their different relational skills and comfort levels with others. Some women have an ease with which they engage others. They are able to confidently walk up to a group and begin conversations. Others are more comfortable with one-on-one interactions and are hinged at the hip of their closest friend. Still others walk through the crowd quickly, barely making eye contact with those around them.

During girlhood, some of us needed direct intervention to get us to move to the next stage, while others simply moved from one stage to the next with no direction whatsoever.

Each stage, from the self-awareness stage to the universal acceptance stage, has a developmental task designed to help us have healthy social development.[2]

As adolescence begins, girls enter the world of *cliques*, where everyone talks alike, looks alike, and acts alike. There is a hierarchy in the clique world where some are more powerful than others. The purpose of the clique is to provide a safe social circle until a girl is able to stand alone.[3] Cliques not only exist in adolescence but also with adult women in the church world. Cliques are normal during adolescence but not during adulthood, especially when our focus as Christ followers needs to be inclusive and welcoming in the body of Christ. This is why some women stop attending church. They feel left out, out of place, and not accepted or included.

Our Misconceptions

As I mentioned in the chapter "Hindrances to Becoming Life-Giving," many girls prefer to hang out with boys rather than their own sex because girls are "too much drama." Women often have this perspective as well. This is a key reason women shy away from women's ministries, and why women compartmentalize their faith. They attend church on Sunday morning, but they stay away from any real relationships with women who attend their church. The mean-girl mentality that is prevalent in our society has spilled over into the church, and it has the potential to paralyze what God wants to do in the body of Christ.

Where does this meanness come from? Not only is it celebrated in our culture as seen on today's popular reality TV shows, but it also occurs when women are stuck in their emotional and social development. When we are emotionally stuck, we react out of our emotions. We can be moody and indecisive. Some of us handle disappointments by acting out to mask our anxieties. We tend to blame others when we are disappointed, and we become argumentative. We can be impulsive and pick at each other and say hurtful things without thinking through the consequences. Sometimes we equate self-worth with possessions and accomplishments or boyfriends and babies. We can be manipulative when trying to get our needs met. Many of us want and need attention on a daily basis. Some of us can be emotionally unstable, which causes us to see authority figures as the enemy and become performers to gain acceptance.

When we are emotionally stuck, our tendency is to believe the following misconceptions.

- We are not worthy of love because people do not always behave lovingly toward us.
- It is our responsibility alone to fix and solve all the problems of our friends and families.
- Everyone must like us.
- We must be perfect and we must never fail. If we share our problems, people will not accept us.
- If we feel sad or depressed, there is something mentally wrong with us.
- If things don't turn out right for us, we might as well give up. We have no control over our lives.
- It is easier to run away from our problems than to confront them.
- If we feel hopeless, our lives will never get better.

Breaking Free from Misconceptions

The first step in breaking free from these misconceptions is to acknowledge which ones we've bought into and then identify the truth. So let's take an in-depth look at each misconception and uncover the truth.

First, we can often believe that we are not worthy of love because people do not always behave lovingly toward us. This misconception feels very real in our hearts when we've been wounded by our parents, siblings, friends, children, or even people with whom we attend church. When we have low self-worth, we often think that someone's rudeness or lack of acknowledging us is somehow a result of who we are rather than the offender's own issue. The rudeness or lack of acknowledgment confirms what we already falsely believe about ourselves. Here is a truth to counteract this misconception.

Life isn't fair. People will not always behave lovingly toward us. We will experience pain from people we trust and love. Scripture is clear that all of us will experience trials and afflictions in this life. Jesus said in John 16:33, "I have told you all this so that you may have peace in me. Here on earth you will have many trials and sorrows. But take heart, because I have overcome the world." Someone not acting lovingly toward you isn't an indication of your self-worth. It's more likely a statement of people's flesh and sin nature. Love them anyway. Love covers a multitude of sins. Plus, you'll have no regrets, and you'll feel pretty good about yourself.

Second, it's our responsibility alone to fix and solve all the problems of our friends and families.

As women, we often believe we need to take care of everyone in our sphere of influence. The truth is we're not designed for this. If we try, we will burn out. What we are designed to do is pray for, encourage, and support our friends and family members. There are instances when it's appropriate for us to solve an issue or solve a problem, but this shouldn't be the norm.

Third, everyone must like us.

Not everyone will like you, and that's okay. That's a tough pill to swallow if you're a people pleaser, but the sooner you come to grips with the fact that not everyone will like you, the happier you will be.

Fourth, we must be perfect and never fail. If we share our problems, people will not accept us.

It used to be popular for seminary students to be taught to never, ever share your weaknesses with your congregation. To that, my British friends would say, "Rubbish!" And I would have to agree. Our messes become our ministries. Our messes also make us relatable and relevant. I have seen local churches flourish when their pastors and leaders are transparent about their issues. For example, a pastor in our community is bipolar and has written a book about his struggle with this mental health issue. His transparency has been a huge blessing to those in his congregation and to the community. Don't get me wrong: I'm not insinuating that we dump our life's problems and issues on those we lead. We need to dump up, not laterally and not down. However, it is more than okay to share your struggles and how you've overcome your struggles in Christ.

Fifth, if we feel sad or depressed, there is something mentally wrong with us.

As a licensed mental health counselor, I understand that depression is real and can be debilitating. However, there are different types of depression, and some are longer and more intense than others. Any time you have two weeks or longer of chronic sadness, lack of sleep, difficulty sleeping, appetite changes, or crying spells, you need to seek professional help from a counselor, doctor, or psychiatrist. However, it is normal to experience sadness in life. Everyone from Jesus to Job experienced intense sadness.

David wrote in Psalms that his bed was wet from tears. God does not promise a stress-free, happy existence in this life. In fact, just the opposite. However, we are promised that he will never leave us or forsake us, and nothing can separate us from his love.

Sixth, if things don't turn out right for us, then we might as well give up. We have no control over our lives.

That we have no control over our lives is an interesting misconception. There is a school of thought that claims fate takes over and our lives happen as they should. As Christians, we are given free will to make our own choices, pursue our God-given dreams, and determine the trajectory of our lives. It is up to us to hear the voice of the Holy Spirit, read his Word, and seek godly counsel for decisions that impact our lives.

That we should give up because things don't turn out right for us is another interesting misconception . . . and frankly one that I've personally struggled with. I am a visionary, meaning I have ideas and dreams that I want fulfilled, plus I'm goal-oriented and like to make things happen. I've learned the hard way that many of my dreams will go unfulfilled, just like Moses experienced when he couldn't cross into the Promised Land. I've also embraced the truth that since I daily surrender my life to the Lord, his plans trump my own. I am frequently reminded that Joseph's life was filled with injustices and seemingly wrong turns, yet God maneuvered Joseph to a position of authority where he could help the people of Egypt.

Seventh, it is easier to run away from our problems than to confront them. If we feel hopeless, our lives will never get better.

For many of us who haven't had problem solving modeled with healthy strategies, we tend to either run from our problems by fleeing or we tend to fight—fight or flight. Healthy problem solving begins by respectfully communicating the issue and working through the problem to a solution. Proverbs 15:22 says, "Plans go wrong for lack of advice; many advisers bring success." When problem solving, it is best to seek godly counsel.

Running away from our problems does not magically make them disappear. Just tell that to the deadbeat parent who hasn't paid child support and all of a sudden finds his or her wages garnished. Problems have a way of catching up to us. It's wiser to meet them head-on from a position of faith and not fear.

Hopelessness develops when there is a lack of vision, when the heart is weary, and when life turns out differently than we anticipate. I have a friend who desperately wanted to have children. She and her husband tried for years to conceive. After years of trying to have a baby, they eventually came to terms with being childless. Hopelessness set in until they were able to reframe their situation. They took their hopes and dreams of having children to the One who loves us more than we can think or imagine. And in their pain, they found comfort from the Holy Spirit and from their church family. Eventually, hope and joy took root again in their souls and they ventured into adoption.

Identifying the truth is the first step in dismantling these misconceptions and breaking free from bondages. The next steps include processing the misconceptions with a friend, counselor, mentor, or pastor and asking that person to hold us accountable for our progress in healing from these misconceptions.

Breaking free allows us to love others freely, lead others from a healthier internal world, and experience more happiness in our lives and relationships. The answer to the question of how to live in unity with other women is for us as women, who lead other women, to see their full potential and help them take their next step to becoming more fully devoted followers of Christ. There is great joy in helping another woman step into her calling, find her "10," and break free from any bondage that is holding her hostage, and then seeing her do the same for another woman.

The Joys of Leading

Speaking of leading others, I want to end this book with stories from three women I admire sharing why they love leading in their local churches. The purpose of telling their stories is to encourage you to step out of your comfort zone, fulfill your God-given call to lead, and impact women with the gospel of Jesus Christ.

Each woman is unique and brings different qualities, skills, and perspectives to her sphere of influence. My hope is that you can find a bit of yourself in each of these women.

Kristin

Kristin Bonham is the Director of Women's Ministry at
Grace Family Church in Lutz, Florida. She and her husband, Chris, the Executive Pastor at Grace, have served
there for over twenty-two years. Kristin is smart, innovative, and an excellent leader. The following is her story:

I never thought I would be a Women's Ministry
Director. I was content doing all my little jobs
around the church as a volunteer and a pastor's wife. For example, I was using my love for
teaching in our internship program for college
students, and I led a small group for women in
my home. Also, I had many opportunities to
meet with women about what they were dealing
with in life. And I could bring a perspective to
our church leadership that was welcomed and
respected.

I thought I had reached my leadership limit,
but my pastor approached me and asked if I had
vision for women's ministry. That conversation
caused me to go outside of my limits. I asked
God to show me if I had vision for this area of
leadership, and he answered. That was three
and a half years ago, and I have been serving as
the Women's Ministry Director at Grace Family
Church ever since.

One of the things I love the most about leading women is working with a leader who has a desire to use her gift in a certain way and giving her the platform to do it. We created a teaching team within the women's ministry, and the women who have stepped up to serve as teachers are thriving. We have a writing team for our women's ministry blog, and these writers are influencing women in a way they couldn't before.

There are women who have found their niche in leadership that they were uniquely created for. We started a "first timer" table at our large, on-campus Bible study, and Janice is leading this table with just the right care and personal attention. She is excited about helping women get connected with a small group or a ministry resource they need. With such a large congregation, this was a gap in the women's ministry in the past. Because of Janice, the women who come for the first time have an amazing personal experience that leaves a lasting impression.

I think if I had been the Women's Ministry Director years ago, I would have dealt with a lot of insecurity in my leadership. In the past ten years, I have addressed those insecurities and have allowed God to be the one who defines me and empowers me. I know my limitations as a

person and a leader. However, because I know
that God has put me in this position, it allows
me to empower other women in leadership and
not feel insecure or threatened by their gifts.[4]

Ginelle

Ginelle Payne is a full-time mom to three children, wife
to David, lead pastor and church planter, and part-
time employee for her father's nonprofit. She ministers
with David as they lead Lifesong Church in Sutton,
Massachusetts. Ginelle is warm and authentic, making
you feel like you've known her for years. She and David
have built a healthy, life-giving, thriving local church.
Here is her story:

If I were to be completely honest, at the first of
ministry, I did not find joy in leading. I wanted
nothing to do with leading—only following.
What I came to realize is that even if I didn't want
to lead, I *was* leading, just at a distance. Being
a woman in ministry and serving alongside
your husband who is the pastor of the church
automatically propels you to a platform. Oh boy,
that word I so much, never liked—platform. A
platform is a raised area, above ground level. So
yes, I was in a position, by the sheer nature of my

husband's calling, to be "seen above" those I am surrounded by. That alone zapped my joy. I like to be mysterious and hidden. But, too, a platform is also a declaration . . . an affirmation of the principles . . . the values . . . on which a person stands. Now that . . . that I can identify with. I can relate to that kind of platform. Declaring and affirming my utter and deep affection for Jesus Christ is in no way a joy zapper or joy killer, for me.

You see, as women in leadership, no matter what way we cut it, we do have a physical platform on which we are more noticeable, but our spiritual platform puts us on a playing field with everyone else in the Kingdom of God, and it is to make Jesus Christ known according to the gifts that he has given us. I find joy in leading women with *my* gift mix. It is not joyful when I am out of my element or "tacking on gifts," as it were, that are not me.

The joy in leading comes when you know who Christ created *you* to be and called *you* to be. Joy in leading comes in the obedience of doing what *God asks* you to do. For each and every woman out there, that is different. God did not make us from a cookie-cutter mold. He created us like a masterpiece (Eph. 2:10), unique and not to be replicated.

Some find joy in edifying others. Some find joy in making meals for others. Some find joy in teaching. Some find joy in speaking. Some find joy in serving children. The joy comes in the obedience of doing as God *designed you* in your giftings. When you are obedient to God, his presence shows up so rich in a way that affects lives toward the eternal, and in that . . . I find my greatest joy![5]

Dale

The last story is from my sweet friend Dale Woods. Dale has been ministering in the local church for most of her adult life. She has seven adopted children and is a teacher and a writer. She is a women's leader at Bayside Community Church. Her life-giving leadership has been honed through a painful divorce, and yet Dale is the epitome of the character of Christ, full of grace, mercy, forgiveness, and love. Here is her story:

There are so many stories that make me so thankful for the years the Lord has allowed me to be a leader for him. Many times as a leader you are not aware of who you are influencing or impacting.

Recently a woman shared with me that she remembered something I shared from a small group I led years ago. The topic was about praying God's Word back to him. She said this way of praying changed her life and drew her into a more intimate relationship with God.

There is such joy in watching others take their next step in leadership. There was one young lady who, no matter the small group, would join if I were leading. After several small groups, I asked her to co-lead a group with me. After co-leading two small groups with her, I challenged her to lead a small group of her own. We developed a close friendship, and I watched as she chose to go hard after God. Eventually, she led many small groups, developed small group leaders, and became a coach herself! No greater joy than to watch the "baby chick" fly and bring others with her! A servant leader draws others to Jesus, sees and develops the potential in others, and encourages them to live for the One who is our Leader-Jesus![6]

Small Group Discussion Questions
Life-Giving Relationships between Women

1. I want to encourage you to be authentic and real when answering the following questions. How do you view other women? Do you easily encourage and support other women, or do you see them with competitive eyes?

2. When you think about the women in your local church, what could you accomplish for your community if you were to unify to accomplish a goal? What could the collective voice of the women in your Christian community accomplish?

3. Think outside the box. What ideas can you think of to empower the women you lead?

4. Discuss the social development of girlhood.

5. What are your earliest memories of friends who were girls? Were your interactions with girls positive or negative?

6. What do you remember from each stage of your social development? How have these memories formed your impressions of women?

7. How did you transition from stage to stage? Was it easy for you or were there challenges? If you had challenges and you feel comfortable, please discuss these challenges with the group.

8. Do you believe you are stuck in a particular stage?

9. Why do you think stages 8 and 9 complement the local church?

10. Do you relate to any of the misconceptions? If so, what strategies can you use to propel you to freedom?

11. Share a time when a woman saw potential in you and empowered you to take your next step in leadership.

12. Share the challenges and the joys of leadership.

Notes

[1] JoAnn Deak, *Girls Will Be Girls* (New York: Hyperion, 2002), 199.

[2] Ibid., 200–213.

[3] Ibid.

[4] Kristin Bonham, story used by permission, email March 24, 2014.

[5] Ginelle Payne, story used by permission, email April 28, 2014.

[6] Dale Woods, story used by permission, email April 4, 2014.

About the Author

Julia is a follower of Christ, wife, mother, writer, communicator, licensed mental health therapist, and Pastor of Small Groups at Bayside Community Church. Her husband is Mark Mateer, Pastor at Bayside Community Church. She loves tea, music, exercising, laughing with friends, and connecting people with their God-given potential. Julia is co-founder of Generation Eve, an online community of women dedicated to encouraging one another in the areas of relationships, parenting, and leadership. You can connect with Julia at www.generationeve.com.